When My Husband Ran for President......
and
Other *Short* Stories

Ruth Harkin

Ice Cube Press, LLC
North Liberty, IA, USA

From Grandma to Grandma

CONTENTS

FOREWORD by Dale Leibach, 7

PROLOGUE: BECOMING A WRITER, 11

PART 1. THE KOREAN CHRONICLES
The Perfect Job, 15
Nonstop to Seoul, 17
Arriving in Seoul, 21
Thirty Years Later, 24

PART 2. TALES OF TOM
Welcome to DREAMLAND, 29
A Lucky Toss, 31
Getting to Fifty, 34
Dining Out with Harkin, 37
Dining In with Harriman, 39
The Pooch, 43
Harkin's First Surgery, 45
CODELS, 48
The Harkin Steak Fry, 1974 - 2014, 50
When My Husband Ran for President, 53

PART 3. FAMILY LIFE AND A CLARINET
Grandma, 75
A Clarinet for Christmas, 84

Getting Hooked on Basketball, 86
With Hope and Love for All Our Children: Photos, 89

PART 4. A HOME IN HOPE TOWN
A Serendipitous First Visit, 97
When Children Visit, 100
Going to the Bahamas for Christmas, 103
Q and Ren, 105
Camping Out with Mr. Fix-It, 107
The Boat as Metaphor, 110
Enjoying the Surroundings in Hope Town, 113
Pack Rats, 115
Hope Town Then and Now, 117
Continuity and Community in Hope Town, 120

PART 5. THE VIEW FROM EIGHTY
A New Home for the Harkin Institute, 125
In the Garden, 128
Vacations, 131

EPILOGUE: WOMEN HELPING WOMEN, 133

ACKNOWLEDGMENTS, 139

ABOUT THE AUTHOR, 141

ABOUT THE HARKIN INSTITUTE, 143

FOREWORD

The quaintly dated saying that behind every great man is a great woman is occasionally uttered in the world of politics. At times it's been applied to the meaningful and storied life of Sen. Tom Harkin, the father of the life-changing Americans with Disabilities Act.

But, oops.

Turns out Tom was not the first elected politician in the Harkin family. That would have been Ruth, his wife! She was elected the Story County, Iowa, prosecutor from 1973 to 1979. And not only was she the first elected official in the family, she was the first woman elected to that position in Iowa.

She also made her mark in the law, was a presidential appointee in two administrations, and punched above her weight (a boxing term!) in the private sector. And at the same time, she was raising two incredible daughters, Amy and Jenny.

She can be blunt. And frank. And outrageously funny. Her outtakes on life, politics, and all the issues of the day can bring outbursts of laughter and make cows blush.

And, Ruth was a secret weapon in the political life of Senator Tom Harkin. Some might call Tom Harkin a progressive. Or counter that, no, he was a liberal. A prairie populist. In a state turning ruby red, he nonetheless kept getting re-elected to the consternation of the state's Republicans.

By training, Tom was a Navy jet pilot. One would sometimes wonder if the fact that Tom had flown battled damaged jets across an ocean to be repaired made him less likely to flinch from incoming flack. There was not a cause or an issue that gave him pause on political grounds.

Enter Ruth. Also a progressive and ideological equal. But in Ruth World, you had to get elected to get "stuff" done—though "stuff" would not be the term she would use! It's been her pragmatism and knowledge of politics and Iowa, coupled with a razor-sharp mind on public policy, that prompt staff and her husband alike to seek her out for guidance and strategy.

The Tom and Ruth Harkin Center at Drake University in Des Moines gives Ruth her due. She continues to make her mark in ways large and small. Remarkably she began making that difference when women's rights were a rallying cry but not yet rights.

These stories are Ruth's. They are rich in history and the times of our lives. And they will undoubtedly curate personal memories for every reader.

—**Dale Leibach**, amongst other things, was the Communications Director for Senator Tom Harkin, and Assistant Press Secretary with the Carter Presidential Administration.

When My Husband Ran for President.....

and

Other *Short* Stories

PROLOGUE: BECOMING A WRITER

When I joined the law firm of Akin Gump in Washington, DC, in 1983, I found myself editing the work of our young associates. They were a magnificent group, all eager, all law review alumni of Ivy League law schools and equivalents.

I felt that I needed to become a more skillful editor. When I suggested this to friends and colleagues, they said that I was fine and that I should forget about further education. But I persisted. I persuaded Jane Malmo, the head of the Georgetown Law School legal writing program, to tutor me.

Jane came to my office once a week for an agreed-upon fee. She was brilliant, and she engaged me in the art of editing legal writing. I learned a lot, and even my young associates commented on the uptick in my skill set as I reviewed their work.

When our editing course came to an end, Jane and I continued our relationship, and I began to write vignettes under her guidance. Over the years, my favorite topic has been writing about my husband—my first vignette was "Dining Out with Harkin." For weeks, Jane and I worked on vocabulary, finding the one word that could eliminate many other words and bring life to the piece in a crisp and natural way. This piece remains one of my favorites. Jane worked with me for years. It was exhilarating.

Since then, I have continued writing, and eventually, I joined a writers' group in Hope Town in the Abaco Islands in the Bahamas. Meanwhile, some of my colleagues published their writings in book form. This started me wondering where all my writings were. Some were written in longhand before computers, others were lost when Hurricane Dorian hit Hope Town, some were printed and published in various places, and more existed via emails I had sent to family and friends. It took a few months, but I located most of them.

I wanted to share these writings with my family and friends. Many of the experiences I write about are experiences that readers will recognize in their own lives. I consider that my life has been and still is full of adventures that allow me the privilege of exploring new territories. Although on reflection many of my decisions seem to have been impulsive—based on pure instinct—I made other decisions to take advantage of new opportunities that women had not been encouraged to consider.

Although I am not recommending that you duplicate all these actions, since time and place in these days may not make some of them feasible, I do hope to encourage and inspire you, especially my grandchildren, not only to work hard but to invite adventure into your lives. If something you are contemplating does not appear likely to be enjoyable, you should probably consider alternate steps.

PART 1. THE KOREAN CHRONICLES

THE PERFECT JOB

My college roommate, Diane, and I had endless discussions about the jobs we would get when we graduated. These conversations were usually held over three-two (3.2%) beer in college bars around the University of Minnesota. Although Europe was our target destination, getting out of Minnesota was key. We had never been anywhere else, but surely there were places in the world where men appreciated us and there was no potential for snow in May.

One day Diane excitedly told me about the "perfect" job for us. The US Army employed civilians to manage service clubs for enlisted men stationed on Army posts. There were several positions available in Germany. One of the perks was an opportunity to catch free hops on military planes around Europe—we could vacation in other countries! It sounded ideal. The qualifications were straightforward: female, single, with a bachelor's degree.

I went for my interview downtown at the Saint Paul post office wearing my best dress and heels. The interview was conducted by two career special services females in their fifties, which seemed quite old to me. As the interview progressed, they asked if I might be interested in working in Southeast Asia.

"You mean Vietnam?" I asked. "No, no, dear, we don't send women to Vietnam. We were thinking of Korea." Well, that didn't sound nearly as good as Europe. Besides, Diane and I had a plan. The interview continued as we discussed positions in Germany. This opportunity was a real possibility upon graduation. I could imagine doing this job, and I think they could imagine me doing it. They would get back to me.

On the way out the door, on pure impulse, I turned around and said, "Sign me up for Korea!" Then I hopped on the bus home and ran into the house looking for a map. Where the hell was Korea?

My application to work for the US Army in Korea was accepted. Even though I would have civilian status working for the
Army and not actually in the Army, all the printed material
from special services came in the form of military orders. I
was to report for a military air transport service flight leaving
Seattle on October 11, 1966. Commercial air transportation
would be provided from the Minneapolis–Saint Paul airport
to Seattle. Meanwhile, my friend Diane went to Germany as
planned.

I was allowed two trunks, not to exceed a specific size,
which would be picked up at my residence in September.
Deciding what to pack required a lot of thought. Uniforms
would be provided for work, but shoes, boots, coats, nonwork
clothes, and a year's worth of toiletries had to be purchased.

My orders called for me to report to work at Camp Hovey,
a military post just south of the DMZ (Demilitarized Zone)
that separates North and South Korea. Although there was a
huge military complex with a big exchange—the department
store run by the military—it was in Seoul, which was three
hours south by jeep if the roads weren't washed out.

On October 11, 1966, my entire family accompanied me
to the Minneapolis–Saint Paul airport. I had never been on
an airplane before, and neither had most of my family. My
grandma, a couple of aunts and uncles, Mom, Dad, my two

sisters, and my little brother gathered at the gate of the Northwest Orient flight to Seattle. For the next year, I would not be able to see them or talk with them on the phone. Mail could take a month or two.

My mother still couldn't believe I was actually going. Dad, however, thought it was the adventure of a lifetime. Someone took pictures, and I boarded the plane.

I had a window seat in first class. My seatmate was a mature forty-something who said he was in investments and bonds. I had no idea what that was, but I listened, and soon enough he had my story as well.

He thought it was astounding that I was on my first airplane ride and that I would be leaving on a military charter flight for Seoul that evening. "Listen, I have a rental car reserved at the airport. Why don't I take you out sightseeing? Then we will have dinner and I'll drive you out to the military terminal."

I thought of my mother. Some of her worst fears had just been realized!

Seattle was beautiful, and since my companion did business there, he knew the city. We had a good time and a lovely dinner, and then we drove to the military terminal, which was about twelve miles out of the city. It was dark by now, and this was unfamiliar territory even to my new friend. We finally found the terminal, which was very stark.

My orders called for me to report to the VIP lounge, where I met Becky, a young woman about my age who was also going to a camp in Korea. There were also a couple of military officers in the lounge, but in a larger adjoining room, there were well over a hundred young soldiers in uniform—infantry going to Vietnam. We were all flying nonstop to Seoul, where Becky, a couple of other personnel, and I would be dropped off before the plane went on to Vietnam.

The investment man took all this in. He said the reality of the war finally hit him when he saw those young soldiers. "I still can't believe you're doing this!" We said goodbye, and I walked over to join Becky.

Arriving to Korea in uniform.

Elizabeth Cox was a rather tired-looking white-haired woman in her late fifties. She was an employee of the US Army in charge of service clubs throughout South Korea. It was a big job as there were eight service clubs. I was her latest recruit. She met me at the airport when I landed in Seoul. After three days of orientation, filling out payroll forms, plus more shots, she was going to take me to my job site three hours north.

She also took me to the big exchange on the post. "You may not get a chance to come back here for four to six months, so be sure to buy what you need." She averted her eyes and said, "especially feminine products, which aren't available up north." Four to six months with no shopping? It was tough to imagine.

We arrived at Camp Hovey, the headquarters for a brigade of 2,500 men. I would be the only woman working here, although an older woman, a librarian, came through every week or so. The service club was a freshly painted long regular building, strictly Army issue. There was a welcome sign with my name on it by the front door. A slender Korean man hurried out to greet us. "This is Mr. Cho," Ms. Cox introduced us. He was bowing, smiling, and shaking our hands, and happily for me he spoke English.

We went into the club, where eleven Korean men had lined up to greet us, many of them also named Cho. None of them spoke English. I followed Ms. Cox and shook hands with each one.

At the end of the line was a room. "This is your office," she said, indicating supplies, calendars, a tea service, and a big book containing the operating budget, business records, and the regulations of the club. "Remember, you will make up a calendar and have an activity every evening. You can call me in Seoul to review the activities."

My living quarters were in a Quonset hut about fifteen miles away. I would be living at a more central post. An armed jeep driver would take me back and forth to work daily. "Remember, do not leave this post without an armed guard, as we have had incidents in this area," Ms. Cox said as she gave me a hug and departed.

I looked around the small office again. What should I do first? The big book with its monthly budget and activities was centered on the desk. It seemed a good place to start. The book was interesting and informative. I had never managed a budget like this before, but it seemed pretty straightforward. This was going to be fun.

After reviewing the book, I walked out of the office. I stopped dead in my tracks! The men were lined up exactly as I had left them more than an hour ago. Oh, my God! "Mr. Cho, what is everyone doing here?"

"Well, ma'am, they are waiting for you to tell them what to do." What an alien thought. I was a twenty-one-year-old American who had just arrived. How would I know? "Well, Mr. Cho," I asked, trying to collect myself, "what can they do?" Everyone seemed to relax when he translated my question, and Mr. Cho went down the line telling me what each man did, the baker, the janitor, the artist, etc. Mr. Cho was the office manager.

"Well," I said when he finished, "tell them to do what they do." They all went about their work immediately, and I stood there thinking.

They had just taught me something about management.

THIRTY YEARS LATER

In 1997, I accompanied my boss, George David, the CEO of United Technologies Corporation (UTC), on my first business trip to visit our client, the chairman of Korean Air. We met him for lunch in a sumptuous dining room right off the runway at Seoul's airport. I was the first woman ever to be in the dining room as a guest and had been told that Chairman Cho would be skeptical of my presence.

It was a formal boring lunch without any levity. When Chairman Cho launched into a lengthy monologue about the history of Mongolia, my boss hissed at me, "Do something, get him to stop talking." Really?

When he finally took a breath, I said, "Excuse me, Chairman Cho, when you have completed your story, I have one for you." He stopped and turned to me.

"Chairman Cho, everything I know about management I learned here in Korea. I came to work for the US Army near Camp Casey in October of 1966. I was to manage a service club for enlisted men. My boss accompanied me to the club at Camp Hovey near the DMZ.

Eleven Korean employees were lined up outside the office. The office manager and Mr. Cho, introduced me to each one. My boss left immediately to return to Seoul. I tried to think what a responsible manager might do next, so I went into my office, closed the door, and started reviewing the club's operating budget, business records, and regulations.

"After about an hour, I walked out of the office to see all the men standing in the exact same place. I tried to calm myself. 'Mr. Cho, why are these men still standing here?' 'Ma'am, they are waiting for you to tell them what to do.' 'Well, what can they do?' He patiently went down the line and told me what each person did. I thanked him and said, 'Please, everyone, get to work and do your job.'"

Chairman Cho looked at me, rose with his champagne glass in hand, and toasted me profusely. He *loved* that I had lived in Korea. My boss looked at me in amazement. More meetings continued throughout the day. As we headed to the airport, he said, "God, he was eating out of your hand."

"We are trying to sell engines, right? Well, we sold some."

PART 2. TALES OF TOM

I was a young college graduate running a service club for enlisted men just south of the DMZ that separates North and South Korea. Believe me, this was an outpost!

It was the mid-sixties with no phones, very few cars, and dusty roads that washed out with every heavy rain. Oxen and bikes were the main sources of transportation. I lived in a Quonset hut with five other American women. We walked up the hill for meals at the officers' club.

In the spring of 1967, I took an R&R trip to Tokyo, the largest city in the world at that time. Tokyo with its many cars, was glitzy, clean, and modern. I checked into the Tokyo Hilton, the lap of luxury. This was quite a change from the long gray winter months in my Quonset hut. I made the most of it: shopping, eating, and going to the movies. It was pure heaven!

One afternoon, I wandered through the grounds of a beautiful Shinto shrine. They were having a little festival with snow cones and cotton candy. The cotton candy was irresistible, and I happily continued my stroll around the grounds eating it. "Say, can I have a bite of that cotton candy?" I heard a voice ask. I turned around to see a great-looking guy smiling at me. "Sure," I said, surprised to hear a Midwestern accent.

"Where are you from?" We discovered that we were fellow Midwesterners from towns of less than 400 people about a five-hour drive apart. He was a Navy pilot stationed at Atsugi Naval Air Base near Tokyo, from Iowa, and I was from Minnesota. When he asked, dinner seemed like a no-brainer.

Our conversation at dinner was fun. We bantered about Iowa and Minnesota, the war, politics, you name it! Toward the end of the meal, things took an unexpected turn. "You know I live in a place called Dreamland," he smiled. I laughed, "Are you kidding?" He said, "Want to bet?"

We drove out of Tokyo, down winding country roads in almost total darkness except for the headlights of his car. What was I thinking? I do make impulsive decisions, but this wasn't reasonable. Dinner, yes, but not heading out into the countryside late at night in search of this "dreamland" with a total stranger. What could possibly come of this?

Finally, he pulled up to a twelve-story pagoda. He guided me through the lobby, and we took an elevator to the twelfth floor. We walked through the suite to the balcony.

"Here we are. Look down," he said. It was an amusement park, and there it was in huge neon lights: DREAMLAND!

Boats are not for everyone, but many are passionate about boats as soon as they see one. That is certainly true of my husband, Tom.

When we first met in Tokyo, he and a friend were having a sailboat built in Japan. The boat was completed in 1967 and they were going to sail around the world. Even though they didn't know more than the basics of sailing, their anticipated trip would take a couple of years and begin as soon as Tom's tour was completed in Japan in the fall of 1967. His sailing partner, Mike, was already out of the Navy and met Tom in Japan to begin the trip. The boat was beautiful, but Mike began to express doubts about undertaking such a long ambitious trip and missing out on good pilot jobs with the airlines. That doubt grew to many conversations and finally, an agreement to abort the trip and ship the boat to the United States for sale was agreed on.

The boat was shipped to Savannah, Georgia, from Tokyo Bay. Although it arrived damaged from a storm at sea, the boat was repaired and the insurance paid. Then the boat was ready for the trip down to Miami. This seemed like a fairly straightforward trip and Tom reasoned that even I, who hadn't ever been on a sailboat, and he could take the boat to Miami for sale.

One Sunday morning we left a dock near the Georgia and Florida state line and motored out toward the coast in a rapidly moving current.

Within a short while, our engine stopped. Tom inspected it and discovered one of our lines had gone over the side and was caught in the propeller. What to do? Throw out an anchor, dive in the water with a knife, and cut the line off the propeller. Tom undressed to his shorts, strapped on a knife, and went off the side of the boat.

He immediately came up nearly paralyzed from the frigid waters. We forgot it was early March and didn't think about how cold the water would be. He could barely speak, and the current was carrying him away from the boat and me. Tom yelled, "Throw me a line, throw me a line," frantically waving an arm. Seeing the current taking him quickly away from the boat I grabbed a line of rope on the deck and desperately threw it. Miraculously it landed right across his head!

He grabbed it and hung on as I pulled him in. He was able to scramble on the boat, shivering and shaking. I wrapped him in towels and then called the Coast Guard to come rescue us. We were elated at having escaped such a close call. I remained stunned. How had I managed it?? I can't throw anything. Throughout high school gym I was always among the last selected for any team sport involving a ball.

From then on, we were religious in making certain all the lines were in the boat once the engine was started. There were plenty of other mishaps that occurred before we got to the Miami boatyard. All of these mishaps helped assure me that I was not sailboat material.

Once, I simply could not toss a line to someone who was helping us dock our boat at a posh marina just a slip away from the massive DuPont family yacht. It was dark, and after what seemed like a dozen tries we finally secured the boat. I went below as soon as possible. Retreated to a closet and wouldn't come out for an hour—overcome with embarrassment.

Another time, we were approaching a drawbridge that had to be opened to get our high mast through. Tom was driving the boat and my screams and gestures to please open the drawbridge for our boat were not heard or recognized by the bridge attendant.

Seeing our plight, a man yelled at me from another passing boat: "Try this," he said as he threw an old tin horn to me on deck. I blew it and the bridge gates opened!

I still have the horn to remind me of the whole trip. Never again have I been as terrified as I was in that channel off Georgia. If that line I threw had missed Tom, the current, the cold water, and the distance from shore would have made it impossible for him to survive.

We sold the boat, got married, and went to law school.

We met by chance at the Hie Shrine, a Shinto shrine, in Tokyo in 1967. If either of us had been on the grounds a couple of minutes earlier or later, we would never have connected.

When we married, a year later, July 6, 1968, in Des Moines, Iowa, we sort of joked that "this might only last a year," rolling our eyes and laughing. Everything seemed so temporary: our basement apartment, our rented furniture, and our temporary jobs. These would all disappear by next year, and so might we.

We organized a small wedding for twelve attendees. No invitations, no photographer, unless you counted my sister-in-law. I bought a wedding dress for $39.00 two days before the wedding. This was not a keepsake that would be photographed from various angles. The only criterion: it had to fit.

By Monday, we were back at our temporary jobs. Someone asked my husband what he did over the weekend. "Oh, I got married."

What was our game plan? We were going to support ourselves, get advanced degrees, and travel. Yes, and Tom had a vague idea about running for political office at some point. What office and from where were not articulated. Children? So far out there, not even worth discussing.

Sounds a bit fragile now that I think of it.

Over the years, we have gone from temporary to permanent. Each celebration of our wedding anniversary tells the evolving story of our education, elected offices, children, and foreign travel.

There were early anniversaries on the East Coast when we were in law school. Anniversaries in Iowa when I was elected to local public office, and he ran for Congress. We and our daughters spent a decade of anniversaries with my parents at their lake cottage in Minnesota right after the 4th of July parades in Iowa.

On our twenty-fifth anniversary, we returned to Japan and climbed Mount Fuji, a 1,200 foot summit, with our school-age daughters. Although we all made it to the summit by sunrise, they were not impressed that we had climbed the mountain on our second date and threatened to put themselves up for adoption. This attitude has changed considerably over the years, and when we told them that we were celebrating our thirtieth in Iceland by ourselves, they said, "Oh, no!" They were definitely coming along, now with Amy's boyfriend in tow.

It seemed just right to be celebrating our fiftieth anniversary at the Hie Shrine where we met. Our plan was to gather our daughters, sons-in-law, and three grandchildren on site and enjoy a champagne toast.

The two priests at the shrine said that this would not do. "This is the shrine symbolizing and celebrating long marriages: fifty, sixty, and even seventy years. Since this is your golden anniversary and you met here, we will perform a full Shinto ceremony complete with a formal dance performed by two shrine maidens in official attire. The ceremony will be followed by a Japanese luncheon with sake. Then you can have the champagne." We met at a shrine symbolizing long marriages. Who knew?

Maybe the beginning was never as fragile as it seemed.

DINING OUT WITH HARKIN

Harkin is the most reluctant diner. Even selecting a restaurant can be a frustrating chore. His list of possibilities is endless in any given city. To winnow out his options, he makes numerous phone calls exploring menus, dress, reservations, facilities for children, and entertainment. He wants dinner to be perfect. "Can you give us a table with a view?" he asks. "Do you make your own pasta? Do you serve Bombay gin? Does the children's menu include appetizers?" He impatiently jots down innumerable details. Nothing will deflect him. Meanwhile, his wife slouches listlessly, hoping the selection process will soon be over.

Once in the restaurant, Harkin becomes even more apprehensive. The atmosphere isn't as wonderful as it might be, and already he's thinking the service may not be good. Frowning, he anxiously searches the room for the best table. He often selects two or three and moves his entire party from one table to another, to the frustration of all.

By the time the menus arrive, restaurant personnel have identified Harkin as a problem diner. His discussion of the menu with the waiter does nothing to dispel this belief. Long questions regarding food origin and preparation begin. "Are the pork chops from Iowa? Are the mushrooms domestic or imported? Is the asparagus fresh? I mean really fresh. You know that for sure?"

Assuming the waiter has tasted every available entrée that evening, Harkin intends to get every last bit of gastronomic information available. Harkin's wife finally has an opportunity to order. "Are you sure you want that?" he asks. "Maybe you should think about it a little more."

Rolling his eyes, the waiter completes the orders and escapes, totally undone. "That wasn't so bad," Harkin says brightly. His wife reaches for her martini.

DINING IN WITH HARRIMAN

Pamela Harriman entertained in an elegant and lavish manner. She had been a world-class hostess for decades and her skills were formidable. But it was not easy to fully appreciate these weeknight eight o'clock dinners after working long hours every day, saying goodnight to the children over the phone, and heading to Georgetown with the knowledge that no matter how pleasant the evening may be, traffic awaited you at 7:45 the following morning.

But Pamela could ignore our realities of daily living. Her reality lay in knowing that good dining required time, skilled help, exquisite surroundings, a marvelous chef with a well-stocked pantry, and plenty of money.

On a typical evening toward the end of 1987, Tom and I present ourselves at Pamela's Georgetown doorstep ready to be entertained in her glorious style. Dinner is at eight. Black tie.

"What's it like to come here for trick-or-treat?" I wonder. "I can't imagine," says Tom as he rings the bell. We are greeted by a butler and a maid who help us out of our coats as we enter the dimly lit entry hall. The butler directs our attention to the seating chart on the hall table. The chart is a flat leather-bound card in the shape of Pamela's dining table. The guests' names are all beautifully inscribed on white slips of paper arranged on the card. It is comforting to know where you are going to sit. It also helps you decide whom to seek out during cocktails.

As we walk through the long hallway lined with paintings, a pleasant little chime goes off near Pamela. She moves forward, waiting to receive us, just as we walk down the two steps into the living room. She looks smashing in a soft peach-colored satin blouse and an exquisite black satin skirt with a jeweled waistband.

Her hair and her perfectly made-up face are even more spectacular than her jeweled ears and hands. Her eyes are sparkling. Her skin is flawless. Her hair is beautifully highlighted in white and gray. Even though she is older than any other woman there, we all want to look like her. She is smiling with open arms. You feel that she has been longing for a decade for you to appear. Behind her over the fireplace is Van Gogh's *White Roses*. On the left, handsome French doors open to her gardens.

Ah, how soft the cushions are as we sit down to order drinks from one of the many butlers. All guests are given the same wonderful treatment as they arrive: they are introduced to the other guests, and they are assigned a butler to be attentive to their needs. Pamela has already decided what we will talk about. We each represent some area of interest to her: politics, academia, media, foreign service, and power brokers in general. She knows us all and she knows what we have been doing.

After we have one drink, she tells us softly in her cultured English voice that dinner is served. As she leads the way, we enter other rooms filled with paintings and sculptures worth millions. Our thoughts of the children and tomorrow's traffic and workday have disappeared, and we follow her happily.

Three waiters are positioned around her dining table, which this evening is set for fourteen. The table is a lovely polished oval rosewood. We know from past visits that it was designed for her especially. The only linens on her table are the napkins. A silver-plated pad about five inches in diameter holds each dinner plate. The crystal wine glasses are two-toned pink. The china is gold and cream with the letter "H" in gold at the top.

Our first course is lobster in the shell, followed by beef, fresh green beans and carrots, and lovely breads. The wine steward presents each bottle to each guest as he moves around the table. The ambiance is impressive.

Dessert is a rich chocolate ice cream sculpture covered with whipped cream and chocolate slivers. Out of the corner of my eye, I notice that great cholesterol-watcher, my husband, helps himself to seconds. Who can blame him?

As we glide through the evening, we realize how well-planned and orchestrated this event really is. The conversation is sophisticated and mildly lively, and tonight no one dominates. After all, Pamela is in control.

After dessert, Pamela stands to give a toast to the president of Columbia University, who is her out-of-town guest of honor. She mentions the Harriman family's deep commitment to Columbia. He returns her toast by mentioning her honorary degree from Columbia. He also notes that the Harrimans' financial gifts have been put to good use. Then she presses a button by her wine glass, and the three waiters appear to escort us to the sitting room. My favorite artwork is here, a marvelous painting, *Mother and Child* by Picasso. A handsome painting of Averell Harriman, her deceased husband, hangs on the opposite wall. We stand for a final good-night chat while ice water and orange juice are served, followed by coffee and brandy.

Pamela bid us farewell as graciously as she welcomed us. We kiss her gently as our coats appear. We say good-night and step outside. "You know, I'll bet you could look that good at sixty-five," Tom says, "and it won't take millions."

THE POOCH

I love cats. There's no question in my mind that they are the most superior of pets. It was a sad day in our household when Tom discovered that he was allergic to animal hair. Our cat had died, and we would never have a cat again. Tom kept thinking that the girls should have a pet. After all, he had pets when he was growing up and they were important to him. "So what?" I said. "Let's be practical. You're allergic and that's that."

He kept brooding about the lack of a pet for Amy and Jenny. We tried goldfish, but eventually, they died. Then Tom heard that Yorkshire terriers had hair like humans and therefore none of the offending dander he was allergic to.

I didn't like dogs. In my mind they are a lot of work. I resisted this new information. Tom, however, moved forward, showing us pictures of Yorkshire terriers and pointing them out on our walks. "Look at that cute little dog, Jenny. Wouldn't you love to have one?" he would ask. Amy began reading about the care and feeding of dogs. After a year of this campaign, I lost my position to remain dogless by a 3–1 vote. Their dreams became reality when Pete Testroet, our dog breeder friend in Audubon, Iowa, told Tom that he had the perfect dog for us.

She flew home with Tom the first week of September. She was elegant in her roomy traveling case complete with water and food dishes. Amy named her Susie within the hour. Jenny's eyes never left her. By the time I got home from work that day, she was an established member of the household.

Susie was darling.

Susie.

HARKIN'S FIRST SURGERY

Although Harkin denies it, he is a bit of a hypochondriac. As a result, physicians have been engaged from Venice to Havana to attend to his health complaints. After he fed a squirrel on his deck, the squirrel attacked Harkin, breaking the skin on his right forefinger. The doctor he consulted suggested that, no, he did not need a rabies shot.

More recently, Harkin developed pains in his left leg that extended to his lower back. We tried many home remedies without success. Then an MRI revealed a cyst on his spine. The Mayo doctors advised surgery, not Tylenol.

Something new. Harkin, now 76, had never had surgery. His wife and sister-in-law promised to be on hand for the event. This was not a comfort to Harkin. Although competent and capable, these two cannot even spell the word "sympathetic."

Harkin prepared for his pre-surgery visit with the surgeon. The internet suggested a multitude of options other than surgery for his condition. And when he reviewed his surgeon's credentials, there was no mention of spine surgery. The credentials did mention, however, that he was a brain surgeon.

Harkin goes crazy at the thought and immediately produces a series of probing questions for their meeting. On reviewing these questions, his wife suggests that perhaps a gentler interrogation might be advisable, especially if this is the guy who will be taking a knife to his back.

Harkin does see the wisdom of this approach, and during the pre-surgery appointment he discovers who the surgeon is: dean of the medical school, head of the department, a seasoned spine surgeon as well as a foremost brain surgeon.

"As you might imagine, brain surgery is considered to be more complicated than spine surgery, so that is why Mayo mentions that in my bio." Ah, yes, Harkin can see that, and his wife makes a mental note to consult this guy for her own brain surgery.

Harkin is dismayed at the 5:45 A.M. check-in. This is a big deal, unique, in fact. Unique in that he observes the long line of patients also checking in for surgery. After the initial check-in, his name and others are called for the trek to the changing rooms and final pre-surgery intake procedures. Asked to strip totally and put on a hospital gown, Harkin strips successfully but gets lost when it comes to putting on the gown. Instead, he unsnaps everything that creates armholes and is left holding a sheet of fabric and swearing.

Just then the anesthesiologist arrives, notepad in hand, to review the drugs he will administer. He seems bewildered when he encounters Tom in full nudity swearing for assistance in putting on the gown. The robe goes on much easier. As he is escorted to surgery, Tom says, "Do you think it is too late to back out?"

"Definitely!"

The surgery is successful, and Harkin is joined by his wife, sister-in-law, and nurse as he settles into his room. His nurse is lovely, and she says Harkin spoke at her graduation. It is all good as she instructs him how to move from the bed and walk around the room. She will return in forty minutes to repeat the process.

When she returns and advises him to get out of bed and walk, he howls, "Why does this hurt so much?" "Because you did not get out of bed as I told you to." What a wonderful nurse! My sister and I smile as we leave to go shopping, knowing he is in capable hands.

CODELS

CODELS (Congressional Delegations) are informative government trips for members of the US House, Senate, and their spouses. These trips are centered around issues in different geographic locations. One of the first CODELS I was on went to the Paris Air Show. The issues were all centered around aerospace 24/7. These sessions were intense: details about various engines and planes were shown and discussed. Then there was the air show itself where countries and their companies flew their latest best planes. Many sales of aircraft occurred at the shows on the tarmacs next to the runways.

Of course the Paris Air Show Codels received the most press in the US. A plane of members and spouses going to the DMZ would be much less interesting. The same would go for a trip to the Panama Canal and many other locations where power and water could be in short supply in remote areas.

But Paris remained the most notorious with its beautiful expensive hotels and Michelin-rated restaurants. Tea at the Ritz and martinis at the Hemingway bar were all must-stops after a day at the air show.

After the air show and all these wonderful stops, we boarded our government planes complete with beds for the trip back to Washington, DC.

The luxury continued as I climbed up to a bunk to sleep. I settled in with pillow and blanket and was soon asleep. I was awakened by someone attempting to climb in the bunk with me. Then a loud voice said, "Strom, get out of there. Are you crazy? She is a fellow senator's wife." It was Senator Hatfield speaking and Strom Thurmond meekly climbed back down.

THE HARKIN STEAK FRY, 1974-2014

Why our annual events were called steak fries is somewhat of a mystery since the steaks were always cooked on charcoal grills since day one.

Our first steak fry was in 1974 on a scenic hillside on Kiernan Farm in Madison County.

Our friend and supporter, Gary Kiernan, had an idea of serving steaks, baked potatoes, and beer on a scenic hillside to raise money for Tom's congressional race. We had about 20 people at the first fundraiser and raised some money while enjoying ourselves drinking beer and eating steaks. We made it an annual event and soon had to move to a bigger space to cook, set up picnic tables to eat, and find places to park.

We moved to the fair grounds of Warren County, and for larger crowds, to the Mueller farm in rural Madison County which could handle hundreds of people. Then we moved to the National Balloon Classic Balloon Field outside of Indianola which could hold thousands. Now we had national political speakers who were President or running for president and prominent public officials. Our largest attendance for a Steak Fry was 15,000 people in 2007. The fry was four months before the Iowa caucuses featuring a large number of candidates—Joe Biden, Hillary Clinton, Chris Dodd, Barack Obama, John Edwards, and Bill Richardson. They all came with their supporters to the Steak Fry.

Over the years the steak fries became an annual event not to be missed. It was always held the 2nd Sunday of September. We brainstormed who the guest speaker or speakers should be, and once we decided, Tom put in the ask. He was rarely turned down. Bill Clinton attended three: 1992, 1995, and 2014. He asked Barack Obama in 2006 and after thinking about it, Barack said no. He said there was some talk about him running for President and coming to the steak fry might add to that and he wasn't ready. Tom relayed that conversation to Senator Durbin. "I would think this would be good for Barack to test the waters with our first-in-the-nation caucus," Tom said to Durbin. Durbin agreed to talk to Barack. A few days later, Barack asked Tom if he had anyone yet to speak at the steak fry. Tom said no and Barack said he had changed his mind and would love to do it if Tom still wanted him. "I think this would be good for me to test the waters with Iowa's first-in-the-nation caucus," Barack said.

A couple of the Harkin Iowa staff kept all the timetables and arranged for the many volunteers. Planning for the next fry began as soon as one was completed. We had a dependable group of friends from Warren County who cooked all the steaks. Then, in-house, we had to begin an advertising and ticket selling plan and organization. We had to consider whom we would ask to speak. The details were endless to produce this nationally known event.

We were thrilled with the final steak fry with both Bill and Hillary attending. It was a great close as the four of us drove over county roads to the giant balloon field with thousands waiting.

A few people hoped we would keep this event after Tom retired from the Senate. We didn't think twice about that. It was a signature event that really only worked if Tom were in office with all the stature and resources that gave him. Also our premier Warren County organizers and cooks were ready to retire. It was a unique chapter filled with memories of hot politics.

Hillary Clinton and Ruth, Harkin Steak Fry.

WHEN MY HUSBAND RAN FOR PRESIDENT

Between July 1991 and March 1992, under the title "Campaign Chronicles," the *Des Moines Sunday Register* published a series of similar excerpts from the journal I kept during Tom's presidential bid—from our discussions in the spring of 1991 over whether he should enter the fray to the bittersweet end in March of 1992.

I admit it! I am in a middle-aged rut. Why shouldn't I be? After all, I like my life. I have been married for twenty-three years to a passionate and exciting man. Our daughters, Amy and Jenny, are smart and beautiful and have minds of their own. I enjoy my work as a lawyer, my colleagues, and the friendships of many. My garden is magnificent and gets better every year. Our family vacations are to be envied.

My husband agrees with all the above, but he keeps reminding me that I enjoy the chase and thrill of politics as much as he does. Indeed, he says that it is on the campaign trail that I come to life and realize my full potential. I remind him that these flatteries of my skills and perceived desires are convenient for him as he contemplates a presidential race.

My mind, however, is on billable hours, Amy's first date, and a weekend trip to the mountains. And I am still basking in the glow of Tom's great Senate win in 1990. Meanwhile, he has been thinking more and more intently about running for president. "The timing is right for change. We need a new direction in this country," he says. "I believe my message is right."

As we lie in bed, I am looking at cruise brochures and contemplating an exciting holiday. He is completely absorbed in a book by Irwin Ross, *The Loneliest Campaign: The Truman Victory of 1948*.

During July and August, Tom begins to meet with national campaign strategists. I myself have a couple of meetings with former presidential campaign managers. It's also essential to find senior staff who are willing to totally abandon their normal lives to run the campaign.

As Tom travels around the country, he is praised in the press for having strong, well-defined beliefs, and for being an articulate leader who has the stamina to withstand the election battle. He calls home every night to give us his own reports. "Minnesota is wonderful. People are very organized." "In Oklahoma, there were a thousand people at a picnic." "Martha's Vineyard was too liberal. These people were trying to get me to say I'd raise taxes."

John Fitzpatrick, a former Iowa State University political science professor, a former Harkin staffer, and a friend, begins working on a draft campaign plan just in case. National political reporters start calling me at work for background information on Tom. Our daughters, Amy, fifteen, and Jenny, ten, have their own views about Tom's candidacy.

"Dad," Jenny asks, "do you have to give up your Senate seat if you run for president?" "No." "Thank heavens. That's all I needed to know." Amy makes her point to me: "You'll talk him out of this, won't you, Mother?" "Well, maybe not." "If he does run, he won't make it through the primary, will he?" "I don't think so." "Good."

᪾

By mid-August, we are ready for a vacation. We are taking Amtrak from Osceola to Seattle. We plan to stop in Wyoming for about five days, then continue to the West Coast. During this trip, we'll decide whether Tom should run. No political events are scheduled except for a breakfast with four or five Democrats in Rock Springs, Wyoming. We begin talking about the pros and cons of the presidential race on the train. I write pluses and minuses on a yellow pad. This is serious business—even thinking about it seems overwhelming.

No doubt about it, we have different points of view. Tom emphasizes the positives, and I draw out the negatives. What's clear to both of us is that our lives will never be the same again if Tom runs. We have heard how a big race like this can ruin relationships, families, finances, and egos. Can we avoid such catastrophes while running for the presidency of the United States?

Spending time on the road, raising money, seeking delegates, and talking to the press are all time-consuming but unavoidable activities. Then, there's my job. At some point, I will have to take time off. At best, I will just lose money. At worst, I will have to leave the firm.

Tom comes back to his most persuasive point: the time is right for a strong Democratic candidate with firm convictions. I do agree with that point. "But are you ready? Are we ready to do this? We just finished a Senate race." "I don't know if anyone can be ready for *this* process, but," he grins, "I feel that we are up for this."

I feel like I am still recovering from last year's Senate win. He, however, values the benefits of having current mailing lists, state-of-the-art campaign techniques, and available staff. We have been over our finances and investments thousands of times, and we are prepared to answer any conceivable questions the press and the public might ask about them, our careers, our marriage, our family histories, our children, and our employees.

When all the facts are on the table, it is clear that we still disagree.

Now comes the tough part. We begin to argue the facts and try to persuade each other of our point of view. After all, we are trained lawyers, comfortable with the art of advocacy. No one is intimidated here. And we have twenty-three years of negotiating our life together, so we are pretty good at it.

I look forward to this exchange. Tom is more instinctive than calculating, and I intend to expose his lack of attention to detail. I am more concerned with preserving our happy status quo than with achieving some Big Picture or Big Accomplishment, and he intends to cast doubt on my parochial thinking.

Because we believe that nothing is more important than our relationship, a few things will not be mentioned. Let's face it. I could make it almost impossible for him to run, and he knows it. I could file for divorce this afternoon. But I am not going to mention that. In return, he won't mention that I could be doing something more useful in life than my present legal work, and this campaign is it.

The intensity begins. Tom is forceful, optimistic, and sure of himself. There's nothing subtle about his approach. He dismisses any obstacles I mention with a wave of his hand. "After all, this campaign is not forever," he says. "This isn't the '88 race when all those candidates began living in Iowa in 1986." Now that is a good point.

Just as I bring up the security and stability of Amy and Jenny's lives, they bound into our room looking for all the world like two well-adjusted children who are happy, intelligent, and ready for anything. "The reason why they are so good," I argue, "is because we have dozens of rules concerning them that are rarely broken. Rules," I frown, "that would be broken on a regular basis if you ran for president." Happily, the train pulls into Rock Springs at this point.

The next morning, Tom leaves our hotel room for the prearranged breakfast with "four or five Democrats." He returns in short order to announce that he needs us! Seventy-five to eighty people crowded into the lobby. The crowd is expectant, eager to meet us. Some have flown across the state to have breakfast with us. The press table is filled. Tom warms to the occasion and "tells it like it is!" The group responds with standing ovations and lots of applause. Hey, he's just thinking about it, remember?

After four days of horseback riding in beautiful Wyoming, we are back on the train headed to Seattle. This time we talk about the presidential race with a little more humor and begin discussing a possible organizational structure and schedule. If Tom runs, we are determined to try to maintain some kind of normalcy in terms of limiting nights away from home. Maybe I would not travel at all in 1991, and we would plan to be with Amy and Jenny over the Christmas holidays.

It's tough for me to get used to the idea of a presidential campaign. But it is beginning to seem irrelevant that this wasn't on my 1991–92 calendar. This is an opportunity. We begin to map out an agreement of what Tom will do and what I will do from September through December. I will run the household, stay at work, and not travel, except to Iowa. He will continue to travel—speaking, raising money, and contacting potential delegates.

The announcement of Tom's candidacy is set for Sunday, September 15. Lots of preparation goes into planning it since this is a candidate's first opportunity to tell the public who he is and what he thinks are the main issues confronting the country.

Because this is a grassroots campaign, Tom wants to be with his family, his friends, and his supporters in a down-home outdoor setting. We decide on George Mueller's farm near Winterset, Iowa, the site of the annual Harkin Steak Fry, and a place close to Tom's hometown of Cumming.

This 16th annual Steak Fry is like none we have ever had. Over eighty reporters and at least twenty TV cameras engulf our family as we walk across the field toward the crowd. It's a sea of people, not only from all over Iowa but from Minnesota, Wisconsin, Washington, DC, and other places. The excitement and magnitude of the presidential race are becoming very real.

At 2:00 P.M. the sun starts to break through the clouds, the band plays, the crowd goes crazy, and Tom gears up. He takes the stage. He is ready for this speech and his 3,000 supporters love it. Jenny has a different view. "It's too hot and he's too boring," she complains, "I want to ride horses."

All things considered it was a wonderful, warm campaign send-off. For those of us closely involved, the day had a historic feel to it. I did notice, however, that within minutes of the close of Tom's speech, Jenny was riding a horse and Amy had managed to find a steak. So much for awe-inspiring events for those two.

Within hours, Tom and his traveling staff were airborne for New Hampshire and other points. Amy, Jenny, and I flew back to DC. A reporter on the flight asked me, "What are you doing next?" "Well, Amy and Jenny are going back to school, and I'm going back to work." "Like, business as usual?" "Yeah, something like that…"

Now that Tom is an announced candidate, he has a campaign headquarters office in Bethesda and has begun to hire campaign staff. The stated rule in all our strategy meetings is to keep the staff as small as possible and avoid the big bureaucratic buildup that has been the bane of many past presidential campaigns. Happily, many people volunteer to supplement the paid staff.

Tom calls in from the road to report one workday spent lobster fishing in New Hampshire, another day spent working on public transit in Los Angeles, plus speeches to the Democratic National Committee and lots of fundraising. He was scheduled to do a workday at a factory in New Market, Indiana, but its parent company nixed the idea. So, Tom got a pink slip and joined the unemployment line, where the press corps joined him. He enjoys most of these events, except for the long dinners featuring drills by single-issue interest groups. A typical day means twelve to eighteen hours—never fewer—of constant activity. And he's no bystander at these events, he's the focal point.

Meanwhile, the campaign is beginning to take its toll on me. Despite my best efforts to be organized, I forget scheduled lunches and meetings. One day several women presented themselves to our law firm receptionist, saying that they had a meeting with me. I am clueless, but when I go out to meet them, I see Joan Burney, wife of the Canadian ambassador; as well as Cissy Marshall, wife of retired Justice Thurgood Marshall; and Myriam Brunner, wife of the Swiss ambassador. They are here for a club nominating committee meeting that I called. "As you can see, I'm not affected at all by the presidential race," I say to Joan. "I can see that," she laughs.

People say the most amazing things to the wife of a presidential candidate. "Boy, this is going to be a tough year." "Are you ready for this?" "Do you know what you are getting into?" "This is going to be a long, long year. I don't envy you." The most positive remark comes from E. B. Smith, a longtime family friend and former Iowa politician. "You can do this. Your marriage is strong enough."

Although Tom is spending most of his life on the road, he miraculously manages to be at home to meet John, Amy's first date. Imagine yourself as a high school junior confronting your date's father, who is a presidential candidate and a US senator! I think John had some pre-date coaching from his military officer father.

When I arrive home from work, Tom's interrogation is well underway as he probes into John's school activities, hobbies, parents, and, most importantly, plans for the evening. After Amy introduced me, I passed into the kitchen to find Jenny and Carey, our nanny, listening to every word, doubled up laughing with dish towels in their mouths. Finally, Tom says goodbye and Amy leaves, rolling her eyes. "I wasn't that bad, was I?" Tom asks.

By November, six people are running for the Democratic nomination. Analyzing the opposition in depth becomes impossible as the schedule of speeches, fundraising, and press interviews grows much too hectic. In addition, both New Hampshire and Florida are holding their state conventions within three weeks of each other.

Meanwhile, the headquarters staff in Maryland scrambles to accommodate Tom's new national profile. The phones ring constantly. In Iowa, an energetic staff prepares for the Iowa caucus on February 10, the first competition for delegates. The other candidates are already proclaiming Tom the winner. At the same time, their staff members are calling Democratic Party leaders and sending letters, and all six candidates speak at Iowa's Jefferson-Jackson Day dinner despite a snowstorm.

From Thanksgiving to Christmas, it's a nonstop schedule for all the candidates. I see Tom mainly at debate preparations and strategy sessions. He has now started filming his TV commercials for New Hampshire. The media schedule is constantly being reworked as events keep changing.

On December 20, Governor Mario Cuomo announced that he would not run for president. The New York call list of Cuomo supporters becomes a top priority as Tom and the other candidates scramble to pick up New York delegates.

A couple of days before Christmas, we go on a family vacation. Tom takes along a briefcase full of phone lists and issue papers. I, however, am going to rest, because I promised him I would begin campaigning in January, when a new phase of the campaign begins. Within weeks, many of the six candidates will be out of the race. The question is, which ones?

The race is now very expensive because every candidate is advertising in New Hampshire. Meanwhile, we do not take Iowa for granted. Tom and I both travel extensively throughout the state on separate schedules. I divide my time between Iowa and New Hampshire, but Tom continues to travel around the country as well. National debates are held about every ten days.

Governor Douglas Wilder of Virginia gets out of the race, and Governor Bill Clinton receives a lot of attention about his personal life, but we are almost too busy to reflect on these events as the Iowa caucus draws near. The demands on Tom's time intensify as more debates are scheduled. I make a fundraising trip to the West Coast for him. The ability to be flexible is critical as we move from state to state adjusting to new issues, new people, different political customs, and an ever-changing climate. I give myself an "A" every time I manage to show up with the right wardrobe.

Tom and I go on a final three-day Iowa fly-around the weekend before the caucus. The schedule is so ambitious—six to eight events each day—most reporters say it is too tiring after day 1. But all the events are well attended, and the crowds are enthusiastic.

Tom wins the caucus with 78 percent of the votes!

We only have a few hours to celebrate this victory before we are on the road to New Hampshire. When we arrive, on February 11, the entire eastern political press corps and our supporters are there to greet us at the airport. It's a happy, expectant crowd—Tom's New Hampshire supporters are delighted with his Iowa victory and eager for him to resume campaigning in their state.

The members of the press corps ask many questions about Iowa, the other candidates, and Tom's game plan for New Hampshire. Clearly, we have stepped into another world where the competition is tougher, the issues are more parochial, and the voters are harder to reach.

Paul Tsongas is on familiar ground here. The Tsongas home is just over the border in Massachusetts, and Niki Tsongas tells me they go home every night. Bill and Hillary Clinton host free barbecues and attempt to put to rest rumors about their personal life. Bob Kerrey spent his Christmas vacation here, did not participate in the Iowa caucus, and seems to be spending a fortune on TV ads. Jerry Brown has a strong vocal group, and there are dozens of other candidates on the ballot plus two strong write-in efforts on behalf of Mario Cuomo and Ralph Nader. How can we make a difference?

Tom and I pursue separate campaign schedules. We will live up here for the next week. Amy and Jenny are joining us for the weekend. Everyday features six to eight events for each of us. For instance, one morning I leave my hotel at 6:00 A.M. to drive to Maine, where I speak to a large group of women at a Democratic breakfast. I drive back to New Hampshire for an interview with a reporter from the *Philadelphia Inquirer*, then meet Tom to produce a new television commercial.

Next, I am driven to Manchester, where Niki Tsongas and I tape a half-hour C-SPAN interview. It's now about 6:00 as another reporter interviews me in a hotel coffee shop. By 7:30 Tom and I join forces at a Concord church for a very large event for women. I introduce him and he gives a wonderful speech. The response is encouraging. I sure hope all these women vote.

Back in the van, we head for another town and another rally, where Tom gives his final speech of the night. It's after 10:00 P.M. as we drive back to Manchester. I have heard bad reports about the hotel we are staying in tonight, and they are all true. We agree that we'll have to find another place tomorrow. Once that decision is made, we settle in for the night and search for dinner in the coffee shop. It's well past 11:00 P.M. and we are thankful for anything.

At this stage, you become grateful for the basics of life: a sandwich, a bed, a few minutes alone, and clean clothes. A good night's sleep is no longer possible as strategy sessions, speech revisions, and media reviews continue far into the night.

Believe it or not, laundry is a major campaign concern. Bob Crawley, a New Hampshire businessman, is Tom's volunteer driver and general caretaker. The first time he asked Tom for his dirty clothes, Tom protested, "I can't ask you to do my laundry, Bob!" "Oh, yes, you can! Listen, Tom, I've done these races before and I know what's important. So, hand over your clothes and whenever you come back, I'll have them ready for you." And he did. Bob always said, "You worry about the voters, I'll worry about the laundry."

For days we campaign in schools, stores, and churches, in private homes and in the streets, and at construction sites. It's cold, the Boston stations are saturated with political commercials, and our schedules have a circus quality to them. In the midst of this, Amy and Jenny arrive for dinner. It's Valentine's Day.

As we compare notes in our nightly strategy sessions, we confess that we don't really know what the voters are thinking. Poll numbers change daily. Although Tom's events draw large and enthusiastic crowds, we begin to wonder if a lot of the same people are going to all of them.

In addition to all the recommended scheduled events, we are doing debates. But we must admit, Tom's message is not coming through. His press attention seems slight. When Amy and Jenny ask to stay through Tuesday evening, Tom sighs, "I don't know if your old dad is going to do very well." "That's why we were thinking we should stay."

On primary day, we visit polling places and do TV interviews. Now we have done all we can. We must wait it out and start thinking about our campaign in other states because no matter what happens here, we have more primaries next week.

News reaches us late in the day that Tsongas and Clinton are running strong, with Kerrey, Harkin, and Brown trailing. We now know the worst. Over dinner, we work on Tom's speech to his supporters. We're depressed, but our crowd is wonderful. It's easy for me to introduce Tom, and he rises to this occasion. Then it's back to the hotel for a drink and bed. This is a tough process!

But we can't spend time wallowing in self-pity or second-guessing, because Tom must prepare for tomorrow's event at noon in South Dakota.

The pace picks up. After Iowa and New Hampshire, multiple primaries and caucuses occur every week. We must rely heavily on local people to run their state organizations for Tom because we can't talk to them every day. This is different from running in one district or one state—we have organizations in almost all fifty states. Because of this massive network, our central headquarters must delegate daily campaign responsibilities.

After every election night, we have a strategy session to nail down plans for the next week. Since no candidate has the time or the resources to participate equally in all the states, we must judge our strengths shrewdly and make some tough decisions.

"Where do we have enough money to be competitive?" is a key question. We decide, for instance, that we don't have enough money to be competitive in Maryland. This is a sad decision because Tom has a natural constituency in the state. We will campaign there personally—our organization is good, and our media efforts are strong, though less extensive—but it just won't matter because Paul Tsongas and Bill Clinton will saturate the media.

Despite the freezing weather, it's fun to campaign here because the issues and the people are so familiar. Also, many of our friends have taken time off to travel with Tom full-time. But the pace never lets up. On one day, Tom flies from Washington, DC, to Sioux Falls, South Dakota, then to Florida for several stops and a fundraiser. At the same time, I take off for Baltimore, then Minneapolis.

The campaign has a yo-yo effect: in some states, Tom is king of the mountain, but in others, he is barely competing. The press is everywhere. At one point a reporter shoves a mic between Tom and me and asks, "Does this bother you?" "Of course not," I retort, "it's the most natural thing in the world." Tom thinks this is hilarious: "Don't ever lose your sense of humor."

When we take second place in South Dakota, we feel pretty good. Now Minnesota, Washington, and Idaho have become key states. Bob Kerrey drops out and the debates go on with four candidates.

Tom is favored to win the Minnesota caucus. Our organization is first-rate, and Tom is well-known. Even a forty-five-minute stop at the Minneapolis–Saint Paul airport turns into a campaign event. Our supporters lead us through back hallways lined with even more supporters waving signs and banners.

"You aren't going to waste a minute when you're in my state," promises Kevin Chandler, our Minnesota campaign manager, and we don't. This caucus night is one of the best of the campaign. When Tom and I split up to talk to precinct caucus meetings in big-city schools, I'm assigned to speak to two.

"Oh, no, we can do better than two," Minnesota State Representative Alice Hausman declares as she meets me in front of a school. "If we move it, you can easily speak to ten or twelve." And do we move it as efficient, fast-talking Alice steers me swiftly from room to room!

Back at the hotel, US Senator Paul Wellstone joins us as the results come in. Tom wins! We proceed to one of the most fun and elegant election parties we've ever had. Word also reaches us that Tom is winning in Idaho. It feels great to celebrate.

On an early-morning flight back to DC, even though we are still exhilarated from our wins, we have to agree that the big picture does not look promising. Money is scarce, and we promised ourselves not to incur a big debt. How and when Tom gets out is now just a matter of time.

The day after the Minnesota and Idaho victories, we are back to planning strategy with our executive committee. Our options are clear. (1) Stay in the race until the Michigan and Illinois primaries next Tuesday. (2) Stay in the race until this

Saturday, the day of the South Carolina and Arizona primaries. (3) Drop out now. There are strong feelings from some advisers that Tom should keep going. "How?" cannot be answered. We decide to stay in until Saturday and then reassess. My mother calls. She and Dad are excited about voting for Tom in Arizona on Saturday. "He won't drop out before then, will he?" I assure her that he'll be in the race through Saturday.

Tom leaves for the Texas debate on Thursday. I think this is his best-ever debate performance. Even now, he enjoys it. He spends Friday in South Carolina where Jesse Jackson has campaigned for him. By Saturday he's in Ohio for a fundraiser and gives the keynote for the big Jefferson-Jackson Day dinner. "I sure wish we had the money to stay in for the Ohio primary," he says wistfully on the phone that night.

Tom arrives back in DC on Sunday morning. He had many wonderful events, but he didn't win in South Carolina or Arizona. It's time for our morning-after strategy conference call. This time it's a unanimous decision to get out. We have a debt, although it isn't sizable by presidential campaign standards. "We aren't saying goodbye," the committee members reassure us, "because we are going to help pay the debt."

᪥

Now we must make arrangements for Tom's speech tomorrow. Tom decides that he will give his farewell speech at Gallaudet University—the only such school for the deaf in the United States—in DC, then fly to Iowa. Not only has Tom attended classes at Gallaudet, but he also holds an honorary degree from the university. Gallaudet is symbolic of Tom's work for the disabled and of what he thinks the role of government should be.

We call key supporters and family around the country to give them all a heads-up. In many ways, our preparations parallel those of Tom's announcement. We are organized and in control. Dropping out of the race with dignity, honesty, and humor is our challenge. Jenny is upbeat: "I'm glad you are getting out because I've just about had it with this race!"

The auditorium at Gallaudet is packed with supporters and press. How they all came on such short notice is a mystery to me. Tom speaks to a standing-room-only crowd.

"For the last six months I have had the opportunity to do something very special. It has been the privilege of a lifetime. That this son of a coal miner and an immigrant mother could climb the ladder of opportunity and run for the presidency of the United States of America...

"It's been about human dignity and justice and about electing a president who cares, not just for the few of us but for all of us and for our dreams and our hopes for our children. Our campaign was based on the belief that America is not some at the expense of many, but many to the advantage of all.

"To invest our national treasure in the skills and talents of the young; to use government to empower and lift up; to give hope to all of us, so that we can demand the best from each of us—this is what a visionary government can do."

It's a bittersweet event shared with friends. We are saying goodbye to a dream and a campaign. Weighing on Tom is the thought that he has let people down by not being able to continue. We remind him that he has done well, that his message is now part of the political dialogue, and that he has a long life ahead of him.

We fly home to Des Moines, where Tom gives his speech again. Although this is sad, there's nothing quite as wonderful as being loved in defeat, especially by those who have given you the most. "We're proud of you." "You did a great job." "You didn't embarrass us." "We wish it could have been different, but we're happy you ran." This is family.

We return back to Washington, where Amy is waiting up for us. We talk about our life without the campaign. Tom will continue as a leader of his party in this election year, but I know his presidential race is over for sure the next morning. Instead of driving him to the airport, I watch Tom, Jenny, and Susie, our dog, walk to meet the school bus.

PART 3. FAMILY LIFE AND A CLARINET

Top: Ruth with Grandma, 1948. Below: Ruth
with Grandma and Amy 1976.

GRANDMA

Before Grandma became frail and sick, she was an active, exciting, and domineering woman. She was such a forceful personality that I don't want to forget any of the times I spent with her. It was wonderful to grow up knowing her. Perhaps you will remember some of the incidents and mannerisms I have written about. But more importantly, I hope this will help you recall even more details about Grandma's grand long life.

My first memory of Grandma is of her arrival at our farm in southwestern Minnesota. It was 1949. I was five and she was fifty-four. Grandpa always drove an old box-shaped Studebaker with a long front hood. Even though I had been impatiently waiting for them, Grandma was already out of the car and grabbing items out of the back seat before I could run down the porch steps and across the yard to meet her. Her arms were loaded with cut flowers and fresh fruits and vegetables from her garden. I helped her unload because I wanted to hurry back to see what else she had in the car. Soap, sheets, and blankets were piled in the back seat. Grandma was of the opinion that we lived in an outpost and needed supplies from the city.

It was amazing to me how my grandmother, Magdelene Newman, could change the atmosphere of any place she visited. Within an hour of her arrival, our house looked and felt different. A pot roast was baking in the oven, rhubarb sauce was simmering on top of the stove, flowers were everywhere, and we had new bedspreads on the beds in our room.

"Now, Ginny," she would ask my mother, "don't you think we should do it this way?" My mother always agreed, and even to this day, I can't remember them having a single disagreement.

Grandpa was George Newman. He was my step-grandpa, a good-looking quiet type with a quick wit. I think Grandma amused him, and he usually stayed out of her way as she rearranged our house. My father, who minutes before Grandma's arrival was the dominant force in our household, was now nowhere to be found.

Grandma had been described to me by my parents as a very important person. She was one of my baptismal sponsors, a role she took seriously, although she never struck me as very religious. "You know, I'm supposed to keep checking on you because your folks asked me to be your godmother," she'd say, looking at me reprovingly.

I was also her very first grandchild, so I had her all to myself until my sisters came along. I also saw her more than other kids saw their grandmothers because she made frequent trips to the farm, and we drove 140 miles to Saint Paul on a regular basis to see her and Grandpa.

Several times throughout the year, my sisters and I had the chance to stay with Grandpa and Grandma by ourselves. These visits were fabulous. Grandma drew us completely into her world and thrust her agenda upon us. We scrambled to keep up with her.

Grandma was a saver. Paper bags, bits of string, and old boxes were stashed in drawers and closets all over her house. Tinfoil was recycled many times in her kitchen. After a trip to the store, she would teach us how to flatten out and fold paper and foil and how to roll bits of string into balls. Nothing was too insignificant to save, reuse, or give away. Her cupboards were filled with jars and old cans. To us kids, it was wonderful to look through all this stuff.

She loved fabric sales. Nothing made her happier than to descend upon a large Saint Paul department store like the Emporium, the Golden Rule, or Schuneman's armed with her big black purse. If we were lucky enough to go along, we knew we had to be prepared. Bathroom stops were not on her agenda. She had a quick eye and an even quicker hand as she nabbed bolts of fabric to inspect. Her eyes gleamed as she carried her purchases home. She often bragged that she had been able to make drapes, bedspreads, and vanity dresser covers from fabric that she purchased for one cent a yard.

Nutrition was a topic of great interest to Grandma. She was forever clipping articles about vitamins and healthy diets. Her children and grandchildren heard many lectures about "good eating habits." "Potato chips are nasty," she would say. We had never heard that any food was bad before. We had lots of fun imitating her. "Goodness, Jan, stop eating those chips! Don't you know they're nasty?" we'd laugh.

Her garden was always large and filled with her person-al specialties such as bell peppers, parsley, dill, and various kinds of squash and Swiss chard. She believed in eating these vegetables in their natural state, so she would pick them right before we sat down for a meal. Her salads were wonderful, always fresh, and made with her own salad dressing, consisting of one tablespoon of oil and one tablespoon of apple cider vinegar mixed with one teaspoon of sugar.

I remember all her meals as being exquisite. She had a talent for preparing food. If you asked her how she did it, she'd just look at you, smile, and say, "Did you like it? It's so healthy and good for you." When her children and their families got together, she always cooked. It was totally her show, and she really didn't appreciate any help. Oh, we could fill water glasses, set the table, and serve food, but none of us was allowed to cook or bake. When dinner was ready, she refused to sit down and eat with us but continued to serve us, running back and forth between the kitchen and the dining room. Despite entreaties of, "Mother, please sit down and eat," she was never happy to join us in a meal.

Of all her cooking, nothing rivaled her bread baking. No doubt about it: she was an artist when it came to baking bread. She would get up at 4:30 or 5:00 in the morning to begin. Her bread came in all shapes—she baked it in old coffee tins, ham containers, and any other cans she had around. She was so happy when she was baking. She was always smiling as she kneaded the dough, put it in containers, covered it for rising, and finally put it in the oven. She loved to serve it to us hot with butter and some of her homemade jam.

If we were lucky, she would decide to give us a tea party. She would find a pretty linen tablecloth, put it over a small table, and take out the children's china tea service that she kept in a box on a closet shelf. She took these parties seriously. She checked our hands and faces to make sure they were clean and then told us where to sit. "Now, I want you to use good manners and act like little ladies," she would say. We had milk in our cups, fresh bread and jam, and sometimes cookies, too.

As we grew older, Grandma took us along with her to work. She was a domestic who worked for a number of families in Saint Paul. She would go to each house one day a week to iron (mangle) and do assorted household cleaning. These families had children our age, so we would play with them while Grandma worked. It was a little unusual, but Grandma made the arrangement seem natural to us. Before each workday, she would plead with us to be nice. That plea was necessary in my case because I had been known to inflict minor physical injuries on a few of these children and break a few items here and there.

Grandma had great respect for the sun. As most Minnesotans do, she craved sunlight. "It's very healthy to take sunbaths as long as you bathe in mid-morning before the sun is too bright," she'd declare. Because we were from the farm and were outdoors all the time, it was a novel idea to consider lying in the sunlight. As always, we did what Grandma did. She would spread a blanket on the lawn behind the house, strip to the waist, and lie down in her shorts. "Close your eyes and lie still," she would command. Her total conversation while sunbathing centered on the benefits of the sun.

During the Depression, a couple of Grandpa and Grandma's friends persuaded them to buy a small lakeshore lot adjoining theirs. The property was in Big Lake, about fifty miles northwest of Saint Paul. At first, they built one room out of scrap lumber. Later they added a long-windowed porch overlooking the lake, and later they added a big bedroom. They called their cottage the Week-End. The lake, as we called it, held special charms for us.

We kids went to the lake either with our parents or with Grandpa and Grandma. If we went with our parents, we drove 150 miles on two-lane highways. When we arrived, Grandma always had the hammocks out overlooking the water. We spent hours swinging in those hammocks.

If we went to the lake with Grandpa and Grandma, we would leave their house in Saint Paul mid-afternoon on a Friday. It seemed to take hours to load the car for the weekend. Grandpa would protest at the quantity, but Grandma usually prevailed. Fresh fruits and vegetables from her garden, cans of paint for projects, big wallpaper books for us kids, extra blankets, candles, and more were all considered essential. If we were extra good according to Grandpa, we stopped at Santa's Workshop, which was a forerunner of a modern-day amusement park. We had pony rides and good things to eat.

As we got closer to Big Lake, we stopped for blocks of ice for the ice chest in the cottage. When we arrived, Grandma would always say, "Smell this air. It's so good for you." We'd smell the air, then race to the lake, hoping that Grandma would find room in the cottage for all the stuff she'd brought. Grandma's food tasted even better at the lake, and on Saturday mornings she baked bread. When she knew we were coming, she brought the children's tea set along.

Being at the lake with Grandma gave us a chance to see her socialize. After lunch, she and her female neighbors, the Solsteads and Olsens, would play bridge while their husbands went fishing. The women took their aprons off and changed into nicer dresses to play cards. Their games were always followed by coffee and cookies, which was just about the same time that we kids came up from swimming.

There was a little store about half a mile away, and as we grew older we were allowed to walk down to buy penny candy. Grandma would also let us buy a couple of O-So Grape sodas, which was her recommended beverage. She would water it down and put plenty of ice in it. "It's too sweet the way it is. Way too much sugar for you," she would lecture as we would scowl. To this day, I have no idea what O-So Grape tastes like in its undiluted form.

About the time that Grandma was making dinner, Grandpa and the male Solsteads and Olsens would come in from fishing. It was peaceful to watch them row in. There were no motorboats on the lake then. If the men got a lot of fish, they would smoke them in the little smokehouses everyone had right above the lakeshore. Grandma would come down to the lake to inspect the catch. These were the best moments of the day, and after we set the table, we'd go back to the hammocks and stay out of Grandma's way until dinner.

Grandma always had projects in mind for everyone. Before we could think of something to do, she had a list of things we could be doing like playing with the wallpaper books. These huge books were old samples of wallpaper. We used the paper to make pictures but also to cover wastepaper baskets, doorstops, and books. It was quite a production because she had us make flour paste for glue.

Even though she had projects in mind for Grandpa, too, she couldn't always get him interested. One Sunday afternoon, she was determined to have him chop down a big old oak tree. He refused to budge and continued to sit with a couple of his cronies talking. She got the ax and walked to the tree. "I'll just have to do it myself if you're too lazy." Grandpa and his buddies laughed, but within a short time they were scrambling to move their cars before the tree fell.

As we grew older—went to high school and college, and got jobs—we continued to visit Grandma. When Grandpa died, she was in her sixties but had never driven a car before. To our amazement, she took driver's education and got a car. Now she could go to the lake by herself.

When Grandma was in her seventies, she pretty much gave up her domestic work, but she continued to do a lot of volunteer service for her church. She loved making quilts to send off to missions around the world. Her imagination ran wild thinking about who might receive her quilts.

I continued to visit Grandma throughout these years with Tom. It was fun to expose a new recruit to her fabulous meals, her flower and vegetable garden, and her control of the thermostat in Minnesota winters. Grandma had convinced herself that anything above 62 degrees on winter evenings was unhealthy. We shivered together under layers of blankets and quilts.

When she was seventy-seven years old, and Tom and I were in our final year of law school, the three of us plus another student drove nonstop from Des Moines to Washington, DC. It was January and Grandma had taken the bus from Minneapolis to Des Moines to join us. We picked her up at the bus station in Des Moines and began driving.

It was an exhausting trip, but after a two-hour nap in our apartment, Grandma was ready to go sightseeing. She had a very long list of places and things to see, but the changing of the guard at Arlington Cemetery was at the top of her list. We went that afternoon. We took her to all our haunts: Chinese restaurants, the National Geographic lectures, the Capitol, Mount Vernon, and more. She never tired. When we were at home, we sewed. She always had plans.

A few years later, she took the bus back down to visit us in Iowa and inspect her latest grandchild. She was amused by my parenting techniques, and when I took the baby to work with me, Grandma wasn't a bit surprised.

In her final years, Grandma moved from her house to an apartment, then to her Aunt Jo's house, and finally to a nursing home in Saint Paul. Through all these moves, she adjusted to each of her new circumstances with dignity and acceptance. After all, she was tough.

The last time I saw her, she was having her hair done in the nursing home's beauty shop. She was looking at me, trying to remember who I was. I watched her struggle to connect with me. Then with a glint of recognition, she smiled and asked, "Well, Ruth, are you still up to your old tricks?" I laughed. Which of my antics was she remembering: punching out the Mendenhale kid or breaking the dishes? We smiled at each other, and then she left me.

A CLARINET FOR CHRISTMAS

Dear Amy,

Would any of your gang be interested in learning to play the clarinet? I have one to share.

It is a Bundy, my band teacher's favorite when I was in high school. It served me well whether I was part of a quartet, winning state competitions, or playing in the marching band in my uniform. We went from sweating in the summer parades to freezing as we completed the last home football game at our Minnesota high school. For concerts, we dressed up and looked our most elegant. For winter basketball games in the pep band, playing in the stands among the sports fans, we were at our most casual. We were a happy team and eager to play for any occasion. It was a whole special social group with a common denominator, music.

I began playing on an old metal clarinet from the band room supply. Before long, my teacher told me that I needed a better clarinet before he could move me to first or second chair, the highest ranks in the clarinet section. "This metal clarinet has taken you as far as you can go," he said.

My dad, who loved music and was thrilled that his first-born also loved music, went to visit the band teacher. The band teacher recommended we buy a Bundy, a sleek wooden clarinet with a smooth and mellow sound and an expensive price tag. The price of the clarinet was beyond the family budget. We could never afford this.

I heard my parents talking in their bedroom that night. I didn't hear what my dad said, but I heard my mother exclaim, "Oh, Walt, really!"

Dad had a truck in which he hauled livestock about 150 miles away to the slaughterhouses in South Saint Paul. A day or so later, he went to visit Jerry at the music store in Redwood Falls. I tagged along.

Dad was in his bib overalls and boots as we entered the store. Jerry was always a snappy dresser in the latest sport coat with a shirt and tie. Dad was into barter. "What if I hauled new pianos from the Twin Cities in my truck to pay for the Bundy?" "Walt, you could never get your truck clean enough to haul expensive new pianos out here, and there is the smell!"

I remember standing in the back of the store as Jerry and Dad negotiated. All my fingers were crossed. I didn't think there was a plan B. Dad did his best. There was a little laughing, and he finally convinced Jerry that he could clean up his truck enough to meet Jerry's standards. The truck was spick-and-span, and the pianos arrived in perfect condition.

The clarinet was under the tree at Christmas.

You never forget something like that!

GETTING HOOKED ON BASKETBALL

Step aside if you believe that otherwise sensible adults cannot find thrills and excitement at a girls' grade school basketball game.

My first encounter with girls' basketball occurred in January of 1986 when I went to pick my ten-year-old daughter up from a game. I sat down to watch the closing minutes only to hear the other parents screaming at my kid, "Come on, Amy, get that rebound! Come on, Amy, hustle, hustle!" I was amazed. "Who are you guys anyway?" I thought. "This little woman with the Brooks Brothers suit and pearls is the mother and I'll do the talking to Amy, thank you." I was stopped from speaking these thoughts because out of the corner of my eye, I saw my little darling actually put the ball in the basket.

By the end of the game, I was sold on grade school basketball. By the next game, my husband and I were yelling for Amy's team, the Hawks, with the best of them. We rearranged our work schedules for games and hurried across town to avoid being late.

During games, the little gym transforms into a room charged with excitement. Anticipation of something wonderful hangs in the air. Parents drop whatever they are doing and arrive in various kinds of dress. I've seen everything from jeans to black tie. Little brothers and sisters arrive with their favorite blankets, coloring books, and miniature basketballs. Amy's five-year-old sister, Jenny, always wears her Hawks sweatshirt and dribbles a Hawks basketball on the edge of the court—just to get the feel of things. She greets all the players by name and frequently speaks to girls on the opposing team. But mostly she keeps her eyes on her sister.

Madame Turner, the French teacher and mother of a player, arrives with her tapestry and settles in. She's been known to drop a stitch or two at the height of the excitement. Musicians, lawyers, computer programmers, and welders all arrive. One thing about this crowd, everyone wants to be there. The game brings all these people together who have little in common except their enjoyment of it.

Pretournament games are casual and can be missed if a work emergency comes up. However, tournament time is different. No priority could possibly override a tournament game. Parents inspect players daily for injuries and give strict diet and sleeping instructions. Vacations, weekend plans, and business trips are all rescheduled to accommodate the tournaments. For example, we canceled our airline reservations for a planned trip to Disney World and rearranged our work schedules so we could attend all the games. We were not unique: other parents canceled business trips and rearranged their work schedules. We were ready for the tournament.

When the tournament began, we attended games on Tuesdays, Thursdays, and Saturdays. When our team wasn't playing, we attended other games to check out the opposition. Basketball had become an all-encompassing obsession. Tension mounted. When a teenager sitting next to me began cheering for the opposition during one of our games, I was incensed. "Get on the other side if you aren't for us!" I barked.

During one especially tense pregame warm-up, one player hit her head on the wall, one player got a bloody nose, and one player twisted her ankle. We parents scurried around getting ice packs, bandages, and cold drinks. When everyone had been rehabilitated, the girls started laughing at the craziness of it all. We parents started laughing, too. After all, this was only a game.

The Hawks went on to win second place in the tournament, and our lives returned to their normal pre-basketball status. In many ways, it's a relief. But I'm still pondering my seduction. Was it the excitement? Was it the fact that so many diverse people came together for the games? Was it realizing how much Amy was learning? Or was it merely waiting for those moments when Amy put the ball in the basket?

WITH HOPE AND LOVE
FOR ALL OUR CHILDREN

We began sending photo holidays cards when Tom was elected to the US Senate in 1984. The cards included here highlight our 25th and 50th wedding anniversaries, the weddings of our two daughters, and the births of our four grandchildren.

1982 Ruth, Tom, Amy, and Jenny.

1992 25th wedding anniversary. Mt. Fuji, Japan.

2001 Amy's wedding, Hopetown Bahamas.

2006 McQuaid's first appearance, parade in Adair, Iowa.

2008 Daisy's first appearance, Harbour, Island, MI.

2011 Luke's first appearance, Los Angeles.

2017 Jenny's wedding, Middleburg, VA.

2018 50th anniversary, Shinto shrine, Tokyo, Japan.

2019 Ren's first appearance, Washington, DC.

PART 4. A HOME IN HOPE TOWN

A SERENDIPITOUS FIRST VISIT

We were sitting at breakfast in our one-bedroom apartment in Suitland, Maryland, on December 28, 1969. It was a dreary overcast day, and we were on a week's break from our full-time day jobs and our night-time law school. The task at hand was to study for finals, which would begin after the holidays.

"We need to fly south using our student passes." "Yeah, good idea." "But where? We don't have any reservations." "Let's see if we can leave Clementine with Rosemary."

After dropping our cat off at our friend Rosemary's house, we decided to drive to Washington National Airport and take the first flight south no matter where it went, which happened to be Miami on Eastern Airlines. Eastern accepted our student passes, so after paying $39.00 each, we boarded the flight. It was wonderful—they served brunch and we flew into the sun.

"I don't have any money. Do you?" "No, but I do have a paycheck from the government. Maybe I could cash it at the bank in the airport." "It may be too expensive to stay in Miami." "Let's see where else we could go."

Once at the airport, I went in search of a bank so I could cash my paycheck. Tom began to explore cheaper places. Looking over brochures at a Mackey Airlines counter, he found a place on Man-O-War Cay, a small island in the Abaco region of the Bahamas, advertising two cottages for rent at $75.00 a week.

The only phone on the island was answered by the owner of the cottages. Both were rented, but if we came to Man-O-War on the evening ferry from Marsh Harbour, he promised to meet us and find us a place to stay. I returned with cash from the bank. Tom asked the Mackey Airlines attendant when the next plane left that would get us to the island. "Hear that engine starting up outside? The plane is ready to leave now. Are you two coming?" "Well, sure."

We scrambled on as the propellers turned above us. The plane was an old DC-3 from World War II. Of the few passengers, one was a Canadian widower who was retiring to Man-O-War. He said he would guide us through customs and help us take a land taxi to the Man-O-War ferryboat. Another passenger was a glaucoma specialist from Toronto, hoping to visit a patient on Great Guana Cay, an island north of Man-O-War.

The two ferryboat operators were also the owners. They joked and laughed at us for bringing our law books along. At this point, it seemed pretty laughable, too. True to his word, the owner of the rental cottages and his wife greeted us at the dock. He had a house for us and would take us there after we had a bowl of chowder at the dock restaurant.

Meanwhile, the glaucoma specialist was told that he couldn't get to Great Guana Cay until the next morning. "Where can I stay tonight?" he asked. "Well, how many bedrooms in our house?" Tom asked. The answer was two. His name was Dr. Keith McDonald. The three of us were shown to the house a couple of blocks away. We marveled at the concrete bathtub inside it.

Once settled, Tom and I went for a walk. It was dark, but the sky looked like a planetarium as we identified the Big Dipper and other constellations. The air was perfumed with night-blooming jasmine, oleanders, and more.

We were in heaven. Earlier this morning we had never heard of the Abacos or of Mackey Airlines. We certainly never thought we would be spending a week in a foreign country. We decided that night that we would explore the island during daylight, but already we knew that this place was for us, and we have been back every year since 1969. Except the hurricane and Covid years.

WHEN CHILDREN VISIT

We can't wait for our kids and grandkids to come visit! We are lucky: they love the place!

As the grandmother, I scramble to get ready, stocking known favorite foods and sending emails to ensure that I have covered all food and drink desires.

Then there is the matter of negotiating sleeping arrangements. We have been coming to Hope Town for more than thirty years, starting with our two small girls who are now adults with children of their own. No one sleeps in their original spot, although some wish they could. We have expectations of how our time together will evolve: fishing, swimming, boating, walking the beach looking for shells, riding in golf carts, and island-hopping with lunches on Man-O-War Cay and at Cracker P's Bar and Grill and big holiday dinners featuring favorite recipes and champagne.

Our schedule is nonstop as we work through our list of must-do activities. On about day 5 or 6, it begins to dawn on us that we have lost control. Some are showering while others are eating. I'm getting breakfast for the grandkids only to discover their mothers are heating leg wax in the microwave. What? They are on vacation, preparing for the day. "We could never do this at home," they laugh.

Four-year-old Daisy turns the ignition key on the docked AquaSport, which we discover the next day when we unsuspectingly board the boat with its dead battery. Because to an inquisitive six-year-old almost anything is an opportunity, McQuaid (Q) has a growing list of items that need to be repaired or unlocked as a result of something that he "didn't mean to do."

The children's aunt rescues McQuaid and Daisy for a new activity: decorating the golf cart for the golf cart parade. They are unencumbered by any real information like the time of the event and categories for decorating, but they have rolls of crepe paper and lots of balloons. It has already been decided that their entry will feature music: the unanimous vote is for some K-pop, *Gangnam Style*.

At the end of the parade, they proudly step up to receive their prize for second place: lunch at the Edge. The next day, the three excitedly dress for lunch. This is an exclusive meal: other family members aren't invited.

I used to resent my older daughter's moves to clean out drawers and closets. Thoughts of organization usually hit her on day 8 or 9 of her visit after she has had a chance to check things out. It starts as a simple offer. "Maybe I could clean out the right-hand drawer in the kitchen." Past experience has made me wary of this suggestion, but every once in a while, she actually has a reasonable idea.

Huge piles of stuff appear on the kitchen table. The smallest pile is to keep, the larger pile to give away, and the largest pile to toss. I mentally object but say little. After all, I'm the one who will be in charge of giving things away and taking the trash out. It usually takes me about an hour to stuff everything back in the drawers once their ferry leaves the island.

Food tossing is tougher to control. Dates are examined on every jar and bottle. Items with expiration dates past three days are tossed. As a friend from Man-O-War says, when you live on an island, the grocer doesn't have the luxury of abiding by expiration dates, or as Vernon the baker says, "You can't tell anything by the date." Vernon bakes bread and pies at his small grocery store and is also the lay Methodist minister; he is beloved by all.

We have plenty of laughs. They are tanned and rested; they barely mention work. Four-year-old Daisy proudly tells a neighbor, "This is our last golf cart ride because we are leaving this afternoon, but we will be back for Easter vacation."

Somehow, they have zipped up their bulging suitcases, made and packed a lunch, and waved happily from the departing ferry. Our place is a disaster: laundry chores could last days, remnants of sandwiches cover the kitchen counter, crumbs and half-eaten candy litter the floor, and left-behind toys and books present tripping hazards. Leaving it as you found it is an academic goal only.

They will return for Easter. We can't wait. We are lucky: they love the place!

"But you didn't tell me the flight left from Dulles! I just can't believe it!"

"Where's my passport? You always take care of our passports! What have you been doing? You haven't even looked? God!"

"Mom, I'm taking my five little ponies and ten books. Okay?"

The only silent mouth out of four in the house belongs to ten-year-old Amy. She is monopolizing one of the upstairs bathrooms and administering to every inch of her body. Happily applying lotions and experimenting with multiple hairstyles, she's in a world of her own, oblivious to the panic below and the timetable she should be on.

I clutch my head in despair. I really should have focused on this trip earlier—or at least before this morning. Going to the Bahamas is the best thing we do, but it's never easy. The minutes race by as we all engage in a flurry of activity. Moving plants, cleaning the refrigerator, stuffing bags, and paying bills all occupy our time. Impossible as it may be, all four of us collide on one of the three staircases in the house. The children have forgotten every step in logic they ever knew, but my husband's memory is working perfectly. He recites all my inadequacies from 1967 on.

Jenny, age five, has emptied her bag and is repacking. Different nightgowns, favored bathing suits, a new dress, and shoes for church all disappear into her bag. "I'm changing everything," she declares defiantly.

Amy emerges from the bathroom with a horrified look. "I forgot my school project! I have to work on it over the holidays!" Her search is on for assignment sheets, note cards, and reference books. Now she must repack her bag to accommodate these new items.

"We absolutely must be out the door in five minutes!" we scream at each other. We prepare to drive to the airport—bags, boxes, and picture frames are shoved into one of the largest station wagons manufactured. We had a last-minute argument over the three two-by-four picture frames. Should we take them? I say yes, based on the theory that we can always leave them in the car at the airport. I win.

We drive to the airport. "I'm never taking all this stuff again! Do you hear me?" my husband shouts. Amy commands, "Shut up!" She and Jenny lead us in a round of Christmas carols. Our seats on the plane are wonderful, exactly what we reserved. Amy settles into her seat comfortably with her headset. Jenny plays with her little ponies and hums to herself. I look at them in amazement. We all seem so urbane, so normal, and so controlled.

My husband leans over. "You know I really love you."

I nod and laugh, "I knew it all along."

Q AND REN

Fourteen years ago, our grandson Q was into everything that moved at our place in Hope Town. No switch was left untested. Turning the generator off, running down batteries on boats, and locking himself in rooms. These events were always followed with "How did that happen?" Over the years he became more thoughtful about switches, even helpful during his visits. Now, at sixteen, Q is the go-to guy for getting things fixed—he handles all the boats, installs dock lights, and fixes buoys. He has the fishing poles ready as soon as fishing is suggested. He has become his grandfather's dream.

Now Ren, age three, has arrived this Christmas. Within minutes he began flipping light switches and fan switches and opening and closing doors. Within days he had locked the powder room door. The door had to be removed because a key could not be found. He loved every minute and had to be saved from running through the house at manic speeds. His movements are quick—you turn your back at your peril. One night he left his bed to join his parents in theirs. In his sleep, he kicked his mother in the nose. Blood was everywhere when his father got up for ice to relieve the pain.

Ren boarded a friend's boat and reached for every switch in sight. "Don't worry," our friend said. "All the power is off. He can't hurt a thing." That was fortunate because he instantly climbed into the captain's chair, put one hand on the wheel, and pushed the throttles full forward with his other hand. He laughed with pleasure.

No iPhone is safe as he eagerly punches widely and somehow finds all the photos to look at. The marine VHF radio is another wonderful device as he attempts to communicate with unknown speakers.

Will Ren grow into the current Q? We can only dream.

CAMPING OUT WITH MR. FIX-IT

We thought our camping experiences might be behind us, but now that we are living in Hope Town in our 225-square-foot efficiency, with a 100-square-foot covered porch where we eat, we know camping is here to stay. We spent the month of March in Little Bluff last year and knew we couldn't tolerate eating and sleeping in that tiny space again.

Our other two small houses were piled with stored furniture awaiting the completion of our new house. The completion dates of Thanksgiving and Christmas have passed, and we still aren't certain when the work will be finished. We revisited the two small houses when Steve and Amy were here at Christmas. They determined that the beach house bedroom and bathroom could be freed up by piling furniture to the ceiling in another bedroom. Now we had a bedroom and a bathroom but no power.

Tom thought he might be able to run an extension cord all the way from Little Bluff, where the tiny kitchen is, down a dirt path, over a concrete wall, and up a set of steps through the ruins of our main house, which had vanished in Hurricane Dorian. Running an extension cord 150 feet seemed almost impossible, and we rolled our eyes at the thought. But by the first night, he had a cord hanging around the door into the sleeping house.

"Of course, we can't close the door, but you don't mind, do you?" Mind? Choosing between sleeping in a queen-sized bed next to the refrigerator in 250 square feet or sleeping in a king-sized bed in a roomy bedroom on the Atlantic with the door ajar was easy.

In a couple of days, Tom had figured out how to work the power cord through a slit in the screen door. We could now close the door when we read in bed. Wouldn't it be great if we could get power to the entire beach house without using an extension cord? It would take a real electrician for that, he said, but repeated calls were only met with silence followed by a later response, "I am too busy, sorry."

Finally, Tom decided to tackle the job himself. The scope of the job entailed locating wires under the house that connected to a circuit breaker in Little Bluff. It was a matter of thinking things through—finding the power source and connecting the wires. He made the breakthrough and the cords disappeared: lights were on everywhere.

We continued to shower in Little Bluff using a cumbersome process. We gathered our clean clothes in the sleeping cottage, trekked through the ruins of the old house, scrambled over the concrete wall, and walked the short dirt path that took us into Little Bluff and the shower. You have to step twelve inches up into the shower, then deal with a quirky shower knob. Temperature adjustment is a challenge. Once you've showered, you have to step out wet and lower yourself twelve inches to the floor carefully to avoid falling into the toilet before you find your towel. It is very close quarters.

"Of course, connecting hot water to the beach house is almost too much to hope for," Tom describes the process of crawling under the beach house with a headlight to locate the five-gallon hot water heater and connections. He spends a few days under the beach house looking it all over and experiments with lots of swearing in full throttle. But Mister Fix-It eventually figures it out. One night we had brief hot showers before the circuit breaker popped. He is thinking about the reasons as he resets the breaker. The explanation is not understandable to me.

We now flip for who takes a shower first. What a nightly pleasure. Our clothes, soap, and shampoo are all in one place with hot water. Then we head back over our 150-foot route through the ruins of our former house, over the concrete wall, down the dirt path, and into Little Bluff, where cocktails and a well-stocked refrigerator await. He says he is working on movies in bed next.

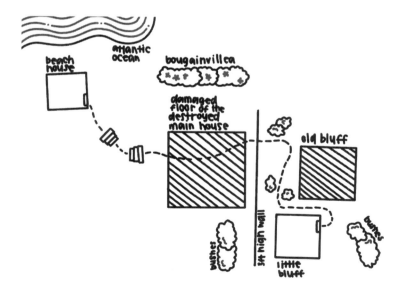

THE BOAT AS METAPHOR

Back in 1967, I met a Navy jet pilot at a Shinto shrine in Tokyo. He and a pilot buddy were having a forty-foot trimaran custom-made near Tokyo. The plan was for the boat to be ready to launch in October of 1967 for a trip around the world. The boat was completed, but the trip never happened. The beautiful boat with its queen-sized beds, Tiki god-carved columns, magnificent mast steps, and exquisite workmanship was sold.

We got married, went to law school together, and headed in a totally different direction. It was a public life, a scheduled life, with almost every week accounted for. As retirement neared, Tom started looking at boats. His fantasies were racing at top speed. He had us going through the Great Lakes canals, down the Mississippi, and the Circle Tour around Lake Superior. Then there were blue-water sails, taking turns keeping watch and gazing at moonrises and sunrises over the open sea. Other fantasies had us anchoring in secluded coves, sipping martinis, and grilling steaks,

As these fantasies evolved, Tom considered various boats for purchase. It seemed that they would all require my non-existent skill set. This boat agenda was not even remotely part of my fantasy life. Among other undesirables, claustrophobia and motion sickness loomed large.

Then there were endless stories from wives who talked about lugging food and linens on board, cleaning up after friends, and sliding down slippery docks and boat decks in an effort to please. This endless toil was all weather-dependent.

Finally, there was the anxiety, passion, and shouting when my husband was at the helm, but maybe I was imagining that part. "Let him talk and look," advised a friend. "Maybe that's all he will ever do. Besides, he is at the age when most men sell their boats." That advice sounded logical, but of course, boats have nothing to do with logic. Tom persisted in his fantasies, so my new strategy was to remove myself from them but be helpful. As long as he knew I was not going to participate and I'd support a modified plan.

Now, the hunt for a boat intensified. Grandson Q, age eight, became involved. His grandfather directed him to various websites, and they reviewed the pros and cons together. One bid was unsuccessful, but Tom found another interesting option that he discussed with Q as he prepared for an inspection trip to Stuart, Florida. Before he left, Q called. Not content with one photo of the boat online, he had found a video by the builder discussing how the boat was built and how it worked. They looked at the video together—one in Hope Town and one in Los Angeles.

"See that little seat up high near the wheel? That will be my seat," said Q excitedly. The next day after school, Q called, "Grandma, what is happening with the boat?" I explain that Grandpa loved the boat, made an offer, and will hear back tomorrow. "Oh, boy," he breathes, "one word can change everything."

The bid was accepted. Tom and Q are now planning their first sail. "I thought we would sail south and anchor overnight in a cove," suggests Tom. "That's exactly what I was thinking," Q responds enthusiastically. "I know where your berth will be," says Tom. "Of course, right behind the galley."

Tom sighs contentedly after his chat with Q. "That boat will really look good at our dock."

You know, I think it will.

ENJOYING THE SURROUNDINGS IN HOPE TOWN

Although Vernon the grocer and Methodist lay minister's Christmas Eve candlelight service was canceled when the Bahamian government cracked down during Covid, the weather has been glorious. We have been to Pete's Pub in Little Harbour, the Abaco Inn for Christmas dinner, No Name Cay where the pigs are, and Grabbers on Great Guana Cay. We've been deep-sea fishing with Truman and fishing in shallower waters around Hope Town, where seven yellowtails were caught and promptly eaten.

Captain Q, aka number 1 grandson, is always first and last on the boat, making sure that all the lines are secure and where they need to be. He is a natural at piloting the boat, less so at tending to the passengers, generally ignoring their requests for a more leisurely ride.

Bingo at Captain Jacks, where we always seem to be so close to a win, is a must. Then there are nightly pitch and poker games where we relive plays and successful bids again and again with satisfaction.

We were treated to a great dolphin show on the way to Great Guana. A beautiful dolphin came right up to our boat, lay on its side, and looked at us. It was so friendly and majestic that we cheered in delight. We also enjoyed beautiful stingrays of various sizes and fast-moving turtles. Little crabs pop out of holes in the sand. There seems to be no end to the unexpected fascinations we encounter.

"Enjoy your surroundings" says our guide as we walk the island paths and enjoy a day at the beach. Then there is gardening, where Grandma puts her energies into designing new plots and finding native plants, trying to capture the right fragrances and moods to embrace you as you stroll through or pause to sit, maybe sip some tea.

The grandkids marvel at the never-ending list of activities that await them each day. They can't do them all on one trip and will have to wait for the next visit. Granddaughter Daisy remarked that a friend was staying at a gated Four Seasons on Bora Bora with nothing to do but go to the pool all day. That couldn't happen here.

PACK RATS

We were pack rats long before we started living on an island. We grew up in small Midwestern towns in the fifties and sixties, and our culture did not allow us to get rid of things lightly. In fact, a chief pastime was fixing things or finding new uses for them: "Use it up, wear it out, make it do, or do without!"

When we came to the Bahamas more than forty years ago, few items were available, so most basics had to be purchased elsewhere, packaged, and brought over by cargo ship. Over the years, this process could take months, sometimes a year. Then a 45 percent duty was added.

It is almost a validation of our upbringing. Don't buy anything new until you have exhausted all other options and run everything to ground with the old. Here's how we do it.

We have three leaf blowers. None of them works. But according to my husband, we aren't getting rid of them anytime soon. He just ordered replacement parts for one. He gave another to a neighbor to look at. As to the third, "I am thinking about it," he says.

Hanging on to everything changes the way we operate. Tom keeps threatening to clean out the workroom, a daunting task almost too difficult to tackle. I suggest hauling everything out that he plans to throw away first. But that is a nonstarter because, as a matter of course, he isn't getting rid of anything. He is just rearranging and checking the inventory.

My favorite is accumulating towels. I can't imagine throwing a towel out—ever. Just ask my daughter Amy. Towels have a long and varied life. They begin as bath and beach towels. Once they become too tattered for personal use or for guests—always hotly debated at our house—they become towels for the boat or the golf cart. This use could last for years before they begin to fall apart and enjoy another long life as rags.

Over Christmas, Tom pulled out our ten-year-old ice cream maker. Its freezer bowl had corroded and was beyond use. I threw the whole thing into a box ready for the trash. "You aren't getting rid of this, are you? I can go online and order a new bowl." Our daughters protested, "They don't even make these models anymore." Tom was not convinced, and the trash was picked up next summer without the ice cream maker, although next summer we ate lots of peach and strawberry ice cream.

Our list of items that do not work is endless. I purchased a chaise lounge at Lowe's pharmacy in the late eighties. Lowe's said it was something they never ordered, but I loved it! It has been moved to all three rooms in our three-room house. It doesn't work anywhere, but I still can't part with it.

Is this reasonable behavior? We consider moving a few items out to the trash. It is a painful process. Our daughters applaud these efforts and begin thinking of other items that we could dispose of.

I am almost ready to get rid of the chaise lounge, and Tom did get rid of the ice cream maker!

HOPE TOWN THEN AND NOW

Although the exquisite aqua and clear blue shades of water, the fresh ocean breezes, and the wonderful snorkeling and boating have all remained pretty much the same, Hope Town has changed considerably from our first trip in 1969. We continue to enjoy sunrises and sunsets, but daily life now is far different from daily life in the seventies.

Back then, there were few people on the island, and lots of open land had never been touched. No phones, no TV, no FedEx or UPS. The internet was in the future. Most of the little houses were in the Bahamian settlement and owned by Bahamian citizens. There were very few places to rent.

The attraction for us was not only the unbelievable beauty but the peaceful remoteness of it all. We relished our solitude. Once our tiny A-frame was constructed we delighted in working on little improvements—a friend helped us add a loft in the A-frame, as well as enjoying our beaches on both the Atlantic and the Sea of Abaco, and planting native species we found in the bush. We felt independent and in charge of our surroundings.

Once we had a loaf of bread from Vernon the baker, (Vernon wears a lot of hats) caught a few fish, and picked up a little island produce along with a bottle of rum, we were essentially satisfied. Many times, we did not leave our property for days. If we wanted more fish, we went fishing. Since we were near the north end of the island, we had few neighbors, none within shouting distance. Very few boats were in the harbor, and few people walked the path that split our property. A truck coming by was a rare occurrence.

Over the years, we made improvements. The purchase of a washing machine was a cause for celebration. Stairs down to the beach, a garbage box, and an addition to our A-frame loft were all welcome additions. We gardened by exchanging native plants with friends and shared little gardens with flowers and herbs. When we left to return home, it was a simple matter of putting the padlock on the door.

In the nineties, there was a major increase in home amenities. Suddenly we had home phones and internet service, television, more restaurants, more houses, more docks, and more boats. More of our vacation lives became entwined with our work lives because we could now come down to Hope Town and work remotely. As property values increased, the local Bahamians sold their homes in the settlement for more money than they could have imagined earlier. Change, which had seemed slow at first, began to escalate, and we realized that ours was becoming a different island.

Since Hurricane Dorian, a new chapter has been written. Houses are being built and remodeled to meet safer housing codes. Property values have skyrocketed, and the biggest group of employed people seem to be realtors. The new people coming in have more money, require more services, and have higher expectations. Their homes are as large as their lots and are equipped with all the latest internet and upscale devices. A two-story house with manicured landscaping is standard. The clamor for the extensive variety of foods we enjoy off the island is increasing as more people desire to entertain as they would at home but in this beautiful setting.

Solitude and remoteness no longer top the list of what people are looking for. Rather than people who can fend for themselves and fix almost anything, many new owners need assistance even with changing lightbulbs. I laugh and think about our A-frame, built in 1981, which was closed-in within three weeks with the help of relatives and friends. When was the last time you heard of someone trying to get a building permit for an A-frame in Hope Town?

We were fortunate to have had the simple luxurious solitude that we enjoyed years ago. It may be gone forever, and we have contributed to this loss.

Hurricane Dorian and Covid created havoc in our community on Elbow Cay. The hurricane in September of 2019 put an end to the group activities we had established over the years. Not only did we not have meetings, but we also didn't have a place to meet because most of the public buildings had been demolished and there was no power for more than a year. Then the Bahamian government imposed a strict quarantine.

Since that time, we have worked hard to rebuild and reestablish the community that we once had within Hope Town. Now that we are in 2023, momentum is building for continuity. There is an opportunity this year to continue where we left off in September of 2019. Can we do it? No, that is not the question; we know that we have to do it. If we don't recapture our former pattern of living now, we never will.

Happily for us, restaurants are beginning to rebuild and return. We celebrate every opening. Captain Jack's had an opening for its bar and then another opening for its restaurant. Although we don't know what will happen to the Hope Town Harbour Lodge property or Wine Down Sip-Sip, we are grateful for the Abaco Inn, the Hope Town Inn and Marina, and Firefly. Plus, other new restaurants have sprung up, even a juice bar, a coffee and ice cream shop, and a bakery.

Every Child Counts, the school for challenged kids in Marsh Harbour, draws teachers and students from throughout the Abacos and Nassau. Outside help rebuilt the campus. Some teachers will not return, so others must be hired. Students need additional help dealing with the loss of homes, school supplies, and clothes as well as the trauma of the hurricane and the pandemic. Somehow it is coming together.

The big annual music concert performed by the students and directed by David from Texas is scheduled for March. Our new venue is the Hope Town Inn and Marina. We will have to shuttle people across the harbor, but we've hired boats to make it all a huge success. As in the past, we enjoy and appreciate a brilliant concert performed by the students. As in the past, we have a spirited auction that helps line the coffers of the school.

Barry Talley, Hope Town's impresario, goes on the hunt looking for choir members. He has a reduced group, but they were able to perform at the Christmas Eve service. Vernon could not be with us on Christmas Eve, so Barry did the second-best thing: he had a service that he knew Vernon would enjoy and appreciate.

Next, Barry turns his thoughts to a real upscale concert, similar to those he did in the past—the last time he was able to put together any concert had been in 2019. He engages a longtime friend to join him in performing on the cello. With Covid restrictions gone and the community Center restored to its pre-Dorian condition, the concert was a spectacular success, reminiscent of the beautiful concerts we have enjoyed in the past. He is already planning next year's concert.

Early in 2023, our Writers Circle began meeting regularly again—reading and critiquing each other's work every Thursday morning, although our numbers were much-reduced. Even though our group was small, we decided the time was right to have a one-night Writers Read event.

Although our former venue, the Hope Town Harbor Lodge, had been destroyed by Dorian, Marcia and Barry Talley volunteered their beautiful porch, and we hoped for no rain. No intermission, no bar. Because we had a smaller number of writers participating, each was invited to read two short pieces. We were thrilled to have a wonderful audience of about sixty people attending. Planning is underway for next year's event. Like many activities in our community, Writers Read is back.

We know that 2024 will be easier as we continue to rebuild our community in Hope Town.

PART 5. THE VIEW FROM EIGHTY

Harkin Center ribbon-cutting.

A NEW HOME FOR THE HARKIN INSTITUTE

We established the original Harkin Institute in 2011 at Iowa State University, Tom's alma mater. This seemed perfect until the leadership of Iowa's Board of Regents changed, and almost overnight—because the university now insisted on only one voice, especially in matters of agriculture—it was no longer possible to do the kind of research and development that focused on Tom's issues and legislation.

It was easy for the Institute's advisory board to vote to take our money and find a new home in 2013. We found that new home at Drake University in Des Moines. It was a comfortable fit where unrestricted research, policy development, and citizen engagement were not just encouraged but were prized.

Marsha Ternus, the former chief justice of the Iowa Supreme Court, was hired part-time to establish the new Institute. Although she often denies this, Marsha was loaded with the skill sets we needed to shape it. We weren't interested in bricks and mortar. We were dedicated to advancing future policy and citizen engagement, beginning with the four chief areas that Tom had worked on during his forty years in the House and Senate: Americans with disabilities; nutrition and wellness; financial security and retirement; and labor and employment.

Our storefront office served us well, and soon interns were streaming in to accept assignments that promoted the Institute and its mission. Within a couple of years, we were thriving, and we were able to expand our influence with lectures, international disability summits, and research.

Marsha was doing an amazing job of growing the Institute. Although she agreed to lead the advisory board, she said that we needed to hire a full-time director. It had also become obvious that we needed more space. None of the other buildings on the Drake campus were acceptable. We formed a building committee and began looking at spaces that would accommodate a new building.

By this time, Tom had retired from the Senate. He could now raise money. He groaned at the thought: the new building had an increasingly large price tag. This looked like a daunting project. We all agreed with Tom's criteria: the new Institute had to be built with union labor, and it had to be state-of-the-art accessible to people with disabilities. We selected a well-qualified architect who, coincidentally, had a disability, and we hired a construction company that used union labor.

The price tag: $9 million! It was a heavy lift, but thanks to the efforts of our building committee and our own $2 million contribution, we raised the money. Happily, the building was almost complete, and the funding was secured before the Covid pandemic hit. The Tom and Ruth Harkin Center opened in 2020, 30 years after the signing of the Americans with Disabilities Act (ADA). We were finally able to celebrate our opening in August 2022.

There are many unknowns and many ups and downs involved in establishing an Institute. Would we do it again? Well, probably, but we are grateful that we don't need to! The Tom and Ruth Harkin Center and its Harkin Institute for Public Policy and Citizen Engagement are miracles. We marvel that it all happened despite all the obstacles, our initial lack of resources, and our uncharted plan. But so many good people and dedicated citizens stepped forward to help. Our friends say, "We can't believe you did this." Neither can we!

IN THE GARDEN

One of the first trees I planted in the Bahamas was a sour orange tree. It was little more than a twig at 12 inches. I planted it in a small cleared area several yards from our little A-frame house without regard to location, but it grew rapidly, bore terrific sour oranges perfect for drinks and fish, and became the focal point of the garden I later established.

I began collecting plants from Pine Wood nursery in Marsh Harbour, my neighbors, and plants on other nearby islands. At first I was looking for anything that brought color and lushness to my garden, then I began looking for plants that were unusual. Almost all the plants in the garden are native to the Bahamas. The Spanish Stopper, the silver buttonwood, the sea grape, and the Strongback are all dependable trees that survive hurricanes and draught.

I laid out a plan of where to plant and designed an outdoor room anchored by the orange tree on one end and coconut palms on the other. I wanted a space to enjoy the surroundings and meditate, have a coffee or tea, or serve lunch.

The most significant part is the entrance, which sets the mood. The entrance begins with an arc of bright red bougainvillea followed by ferns, pineapples, jasmine, always blooming red ixoras, and yellow oleanders growing 7 feet tall. Scents are everywhere as you begin walking the graveled paths loaded with wall-to-wall lush plants.

One of my favorites is the powder puff bush. One morning, red berries will begin to appear on the bush. They look similar to raspberries, but within a day or two, they abandon their form and explode into powder puffs.

Follow the path to the left, and behind a group of flowering hibiscus and bamboo is a Japanese tea house. The inside is complete with a table, pillows and benches for the less flexible. As you drink tea you are facing a big bubbling fountain surrounded by tall Bridal Bouquet trees complete with an overwhelming scent of lily.

Now you are in a room removed from any outside road noise and electronic equipment. The bubbling water fountain and an occasional bee buzzing are the only sounds in this sanctuary.

The tea house.

Two views in the garden.

VACATIONS

We agree. It is mandatory to have tickets for our next trip scheduled or at least a specific plan in mind.

The anticipation of travel can be thrilling, especially when considering and learning about new places, but a spur-of-the-moment trip isn't a bad venture either.

I like returning to favored countries on a regular basis. Japan and France are at the top of the list requiring repeat visits,

Once Tom took me on a surprise trip, asking me to meet him at an airport. He told me the temperature at our destination and that I needed to wear cowboy boots. I couldn't guess the location—it was Las Vegas to meet Robert Redford and Jane Fonda filming a movie outside the city.

Another time I insisted Tom revisit Petra with me. I had been there as part of a business trip and this ancient archaeological city was so unique and spectacular, I knew he had to see it. We traveled together to the desert in southern Jordon to tour Petra.

But, nothing beats the spontaneity of our trip to head to Washington National airport one early morning after Christmas and take the first flight south. We ended up in the Abacos in the Bahamas at the end of a long day eating fish chowder on a small island we had never heard of that morning.

With an attitude that anything can happen, and always open to suggestion, I keep my passport in my handbag.

Ruth sworn in to OPIC by United States Attorney
General Janet Reno with Tom.

EPILOGUE: WOMEN HELPING WOMEN

In August of 2018 I was inducted into the Iowa Women's Hall of Fame, sponsored by the Iowa Commission on the Status of Women, at the State Historical Society building in Des Moines. This is the speech I gave at the ceremony.

Thank you for your kind and generous words! I am thrilled to be honored by the Iowa Commission on the Status of Women, which has been such an effective voice for women in our state. I want to thank my husband, sister, aunt, cousin, and niece for traveling to be with me today. Also, thanks to so many good friends who are here today.

Women recognizing women, helping women, and celebrating women has been a passion of mine throughout my life.

My first job was chopping corn out of beans in rural Minnesota. I was fourteen and had to ask for the job, and I have been working at something ever since. I am among the first generation of women who pursued full-time careers outside the home and juggled career and family life. It was a debate among us, and many promising and well-educated women decided not to risk it—especially if it was not the economic necessity it increasingly is today.

Early on, I was motivated by a couple of guidelines. One, you have to be in the room to make a difference. A second guideline was to do what I wanted to do. Most of the work and jobs I have done, people told me I couldn't do. I never listened to them. This has been liberating.

As a lawyer just out of law school, I was hired to work as a legal aid lawyer in Polk County beginning in November of 1972. In May, as I was studying for the Iowa bar exam, the Story County Democratic Chair came to our house in Ames. Story County Democrats were notorious for not filling the ticket for county offices. She wanted to change that, and she asked me to fill the slot of county attorney. "I haven't even passed the bar yet, and besides I am going to be a legal aid attorney," I protested.

"That, my dear, is irrelevant. You couldn't possibly win this race. There are no women county attorneys in any of the ninety-nine counties, and in Story County there are no women attorneys except you. Not to mention that Story County in over a hundred years of existence has only elected one Democrat, who was promptly defeated two years later. I am just asking you to help fill the ticket."

That pretty well nailed it, and I said, "Sure, sign me up." Well, against all odds, I won! The attorney general sent us letters titled "Lady and gentlemen."

I was now in the room, and it was a very good room, but I determined from the start that other women join me. Happily, more women began attending Iowa law schools in the seventies. A male student once said to me, "I would really like to intern with you, but I hear you only hire women." "That is absolutely true. I am the only woman out of ninety-nine. If I don't hire women, who will?"

Over the next six years, women began joining the prosecutor ranks. My sister Sherry graduated from the University of Minnesota law school and became Winneshiek County's first female assistant county attorney. When I completed my two terms, another woman succeeded me, and since 1972 women have been in the prosecutors' rooms throughout our state.

When I moved to Washington, DC, to join my husband with our three-year-old daughter, Amy—daughter Jenny was born two-and-a-half years later—I was told that whereas I might be a big deal in Iowa, my résumé did not translate to a federal-level job. I became deputy general counsel at the Department of Agriculture. The secretary said he didn't want me. "When I look at you, I see my wife, and she could never do this job." I took the job anyway. After a couple of months, he apologized to me and said he had been wrong, and we became pals.

During my tenure, I got a call one day from the United States Office of the General Counsel in the vice president's office. "I see that you have lawyers working part-time in your office." "Yes, we have some extremely talented women lawyers who are mothers or becoming mothers. They are a bit daunted by parenting, work, traffic, and child care but don't want to leave the workforce, so I agreed they could work part-time."

"Well, no one else is doing this in any of the other general counsel offices." "It isn't against federal regulations, is it?" I asked. "Well, no." "That's a good thing then, isn't it? I will keep doing it."

I was offered a presidential appointment to become president and CEO of the Overseas Private Investment Corporation (OPIC) in 1993. Comprised of lawyers and bankers, this is an independent federal agency that promotes and supports private sector business investments around the world in politically unstable countries. No woman had ever headed this organization. OPIC did business with chief financial officers, heads of US corporations, and heads of state around the world—all men. But I had a big advantage: I had the authority and the money.

We were wildly successful by any measure due to our talented team, support from the White House, and newly expanded jurisdiction, primarily because of the breakup of the Soviet Union. But the statistic I liked best was at the end of four years, 50 percent of our lawyers were women and 50 percent of our bankers were women.

Corporate America can be a difficult culture for women because there are so few at or near the top. I was offered a wonderful opportunity by a just-appointed chairman and CEO of a long-established New England corporation. Honestly, I thought I was on another planet. No woman had ever been part of senior management or had a direct report to the chairman.

I was told that even though I was now in the inner circle of senior management, they were not interested in bringing in more women at my level. I could hire women if I wanted, but that was it! It was tough, but I am delighted to know that within our worldwide corporate network, many capable women have achieved high-ranking executive positions within the businesses, some from Iowa.

One moment does stand out. I was boarding one of our corporate helicopters in Hartford to fly to New York for a meeting. I walked over to meet the pilot and copilot on the tarmac. They turned around. They were beaming. They were women! "Mrs. Harkin, what do you think? It's just the three of us." I loved it! And I smiled all the way to New York.

Now we are in this room. It's the right place. I am looking at my thirty-three-year-old lawyer niece, Carrie. She is in the room. Like many of her generation, and our own daughters, she works full-time, is raising a family, maintains a household with her husband, and she is helping women. They get it!

Women helping women.

Thank you again for this recognition.

ACKNOWLEDGEMENTS AND SPECIAL THANKS

I want to especially thank the members of the Hope Town Writers Circle for their support in encouraging my writing over the years. Collectively, their candid critiques of my writings have been invaluable. Our post-Hurricane Dorian membership has also been encouraging in writing this little book of my vignettes.

Many friends and family from Iowa and the DC area have cheered me on, offering suggestions on topics, photos, and even the title from Richard Gilbert.

Special thanks to Dale Leibach, and Patty Beneke for their editing and generosity in time spent reviewing and revising the vignettes. A big thank you to Ice Cube Press publisher Steve Semken for believing in the success of this book and always keeping a sense of humor.

I am grateful to my grandson Luke Harkin Goodrich for providing me with his wonderful sketches. For one of his maps, he came to Hope Town and walked the route to get it accurate.

Special thanks to my daughters and grandchildren for their inspiration in compelling me to write about them. They are all a delight that continues to make me laugh and smile.

I am very grateful for my favorite subject, my husband. He continues to provide never-ending topics of adventures and misadventures. He has always supported my writing even though not all of it shows him at his best.

Finally, I want to thank the staff and supporters of the Harkin Institute. For Tom and for me, we have made the work of the Institute our highest calling. We have made remarkable progress in advancing the tenets of the Americans With Disabilities Act to countries around the world. We still have much work ahead.

I hope you will enjoy this collection of stories. A portion of the proceeds will go to supporting the mission of the Harkin Institute. I also hope you will visit the Tom and Ruth Harkin Center where the Institute is housed on the Drake University campus.

Ruth Harkin has enjoyed a diverse career working for the US Government, Iowa State Government, county government, corporations, nonprofit organizations, the law, and academe. She was elected county attorney of Story County, Iowa, in 1973 and served until 1979. From 1979 to 1981, she served as a deputy counsel for the United States Department of Agriculture prior to joining the Washington law firm of Akin Gump Strauss Hauer & Feld, LLP in 1983. In 1993, President Bill Clinton named her Chair and Chief Executive Officer of the Overseas Private Investment Corporation (OPIC). Harkin left the government and became Senior Vice President for international affairs and government relations of United Technologies in April 1997. In 2002, she became a Director of ConocoPhillips. Harkin was a member of the Iowa Board of Regents from 2005 to 2015. She was inducted into the Iowa Women's Hall of Fame in 2018. She continues to serve on various nonprofit boards including the National Advisory Committee of the Harkin Institute.

The Harkin Institute
CONNECTING PEOPLE WITH POLICY

The Tom and Ruth Harkin Center, home of The Harkin Institute, opened in 2020, thirty years after the signing of the Americans with Disabilities Act (ADA), and is a model of accessibility. The Center exemplifies the concept of Universal Design, which expands design beyond base accessibility requirements of the ADA and creates a truly inclusive setting, understandable and accessible by all people.

There are many ways to make a charitable gift to the Institute. Making a commitment today provides a powerful endorsement and insures its long-term success. All money will be used to support research, scholarship, forums, and lectures. All author proceeds from *When My Husband Ran for President and Other Short Stories* will be contributed to The Harkin Institute Endowment. FMI: www.harkininstitute. drake.edu

THE HARKIN INSTITUTE FOR PUBLIC POLICY & CITIZEN ENGAGEMENT

at Drake University was founded on the premise that good public policy is best achieved when policymakers have access to high quality information, political processes are open and well-understood, and citizens are informed and active participants. To encourage fact-based policy decisions and the active engagement of citizens in the formation of public policy, The Harkin Institute provides:

► **DATA-DRIVEN ANALYSIS AND RESEARCH.** The Institute pursues an evidence-based, nonpartisan research agenda to provide policymakers and citizens access to high-quality information on the social justice issues to which Senator Tom Harkin devoted his career, including people with disabilities, labor and employment, retirement security, and wellness and nutrition.

► **EDUCATION.** Institute staff members educate stakeholders on these issues and inform public opinion by serving as expert resources and sharing valuable research and information via publications, social media, and other channels.

► **OUTREACH.** The Institute facilitates public programming that engages thought leaders and citizens in the discussion and formulation of public policy, including the annual Harkin International Disability Employment Summit, which gathers private employers, government leaders and disability advocates from more than forty countries to address barriers to competitive, integrated employment for persons with disabilities.

The Ice Cube Press began publishing in 1991 to focus on how to live with the natural world and to better understand how people can best live together in the communities they share and inhabit. Using the literary arts to explore life and experiences in the heartland of the United States we have been recognized by so many well-known writers including: Bill Bradley, Gary Snyder, Gene Logsdon, Wes Jackson, Patricia Hampl, Greg Brown, Jim Harrison, Annie Dillard, Ken Burns, Roz Chast, Jane Hamilton, Daniel Menaker, Kathleen Norris, Janisse Ray, Craig Lesley, Alison Deming, Harriet Lerner, Richard Lynn Stegner, Richard Rhodes, Michael Pollan, David Abram, David Orr, and Barry Lopez. We've published a number of well-known authors including: Mary Swander, Jim Heynen, Mary Pipher, Bill Holm, Connie Mutel, John T. Price, Carol Bly, Marvin Bell, Debra Marquart, Ted Kooser, Stephanie Mills, Bill McKibben, Craig Lesley, Elizabeth McCracken, Derrick Jensen, Dean Bakopoulos, Rick Bass, Linda Hogan, Pam Houston, and Paul Gruchow. Check out Ice Cube Press books on our web site, join our email list, Facebook group, or follow us on X/Twitter. Visit booksellers, museum shops, or any place you can find good books and support our truly honest to goodness independent publishing projects and discover why we continue striving to hear the other side.

Ice Cube Press, LLC (Est. 1991)
North Liberty, Iowa, Midwest, USA
Resting above the Silurian and Jordan aquifers
steve@icecubepress.com
Check us out on X/Twitter and Facebook.
Order direct: www.icecubepress.com
Subscribe to our Substack: *Publishing, Writing, and Smart Life Secrets*

Celebrating Over Thirty Years of Independent Publishing

To Fenna Marie—
May my best stories pass to you
may you continue to glow and grow
in many more stories of joy.